The Entrepreneurial Ben Franklin

His Life, Failures, and
Ultimate Successes
in the World of Business

James Charles Bouffard, Psy.D., Ph.D.

(Edited by: Lisa Diane Branscome)

Third Edition

Illustrated

Lynn Paulo Foundation
Pomona, California

ISBN 978-0-578-01259-9

Printed in the United States of America

Other works by Dr. Bouffard:

Be A Private Investigator
The Magician's Fight!
A Quest For Absolute Power
DEFIANCE! A Saga of David Crockett and the Alamo
Doc Jim's Book of WHO CARES!? (trivia facts)

Dedicated to:
Lisa Diane Branscome

I hope she remembers our work together,
long into the future.

Acknowledgments

The author gratefully acknowledges Massachusetts Institute of Technology, U.S. National Archives and Records Administration, U. S. National Park Service, American Philosophical Society, Metropolitan Museum of Art, Library Company of Philadelphia, the Library of Congress and National Historic Landmark, NRHP reference #71000565 [the Owls Nest — Lake George, New York estate of Edward Eggleston] for needed information and kind permission to reproduce illustrations within this work.

To the staff of the Los Angeles Public Library, the library of UCLA and the smaller yet no less informative libraries of Claremont, Pomona and Ontario, California for their amiable assistance and extreme patience, my gratitude is extended beyond mere appreciation.

Preface

Should Benjamin Franklin excite your search for knowledge, this is quite possibly the smallest volume you may ever read. Still, it is packed with months of exhaustive research. Its brevity is an attempt to accord you a clear narrative of a man who was as much an enigma in his own time as he is today.

Historical records, documents, biographies, and several edited versions of Franklin's autobiographies were scanned and re-scanned for accuracy. Where contradictions arose between various authors, cross-referencing decided true facts.

Quotations in this work are from original scripts, letters and documents; with neither grammar, spelling nor punctuation changed. Exceptions are the archaic fashion of capitalizing the first letter of nearly every other word in a sentence. I took the liberty, for a better understanding of meaning, to dispense with this outmoded form of writing.

Though merely a subject of long-faded history in my elementary schooling, by the time I felt prepared to pen *The Entrepreneurial Ben Franklin*'s initial draft, Ben and I had become friends. It is my sincere hope you feel the same after its reading.

Dr. James Charles Bouffard
Pomona, California
October 20, 2008

Contents

Contents

Illustrations List

Following page 88:

- Captain John Bonner's map of Boston, 1722...
- Ben Franklin's birthplace on 17 Milk Street...
- Ben at work as apprentice to his brother James...
- The plaque in this photo reads...
- When Ben entered Philadelphia on Sunday...
- Ben's shop on High Street [now Market Street]...
- Ben makes notes for *Poor Richard's*, ca 1740...
- Deborah Read Rogers Franklin, ca 1766...
- Ben Franklin's famous kite experiment of 1752...
- William Franklin, ca 1793...
- Benjamin Franklin at the Court of Versailles, France, ca 1777...
- Benjamin Franklin, ca 1780...
- Sarah Franklin Bache [called Sally]...
- The Philadelphia Library moved into...
- Ben rests at Christ Church Burial Ground...

Following page 162:

- Young Ben Franklin stands notice by provincial...

Prologue

In the fall of 1776, General George Washington ordered his troops to retreat from Long Island. England's well-equipped forces, outnumbering his frayed army two-to-one, had taken possession of New York.

Within the past week, American General Benedict Arnold had backed out of Canada in humiliated defeat.

The war for independence was going badly. The colonies had very little money, no credit, few munitions factories, no fleets, and a small number of trained officers. Their need for outside help was clearly evident.

France prepared to secretly ship arms for colonial use, but required some show of strength before committing themselves.

England and France were natural enemies evolving from ancient conflicts, and a logical alliance between America and France brewed in the colonies since 1775. Yet the French monarchy hesitated. To back a virgin country having no chance to grow of its own would constitute political suicide. Unless "...the new state gives signs of strength," she would hold back.

Seventy-year-old Dr. Benjamin Franklin, oldest member in the Continental Congress, visited General Washington at his headquarters in Cambridge, Massachusetts. He was accompanied by Silas Deane and Dr. Arthur Lee.

They were shown maps, plans, and tactics for victory. Washington spared no inducement. "This war can be ours," he stared into the older man's eyes, "if...we have the resources! We must prove our worth to France! Without her help, all could be lost!"

Franklin agreed, and he, with and his two fellow delegates, was soon off to the Court of Versailles.

On December 26, 1776, Washington soundly thrashed the British-Hessian garrison in the Battle of Trenton, followed by General Horatio Gates' victory over the English General Burgoyne at Saratoga.

France took notice.

Calling Franklin to court, Louis XVI offered to consign to the colonies, while negotiating a treaty, certain requisitioned supplies.

In February of 1778, the Treaty of Alliance was signed to the applause of Parisian society. Their American hero, "*Bonhomme* [1] *Richard*," had done it. His prevalence over King Louis XVI and his queen, Marie Antoinette, was a feat no Frenchman could have hoped to accomplish.

Prologue

Although history credits the victorious battles of Trenton and Saratoga as paving the way for the Treaty of Alliance, as well as the Treaty of Amity and Commerce, Franklin's skill as a diplomat played a major role. He knew when to stress his points, and when to lay back. He also knew that "for one to endear a foreign nation to one's cause, one must embrace her people and her ways."

Where colonial America deemed it sinful to display idleness, France thought it vulgar to look busy. Where the stately John Adams criticized Franklin's "lust for pleasure," France adored his "love of pleasure and casual ways." As one young French government official wrote: "He [Franklin] eats, sleeps, works whenever he sees fit... There never was such a leisurely man, tho' he handles a tremendous amount of business. No matter when one asks for him, he is always available."

This was Benjamin Franklin, the diplomat. Loved by most of the world, even today.

But what we are about to unfold is the story of Ben Franklin, the entrepreneur. A young man, not so well-loved at times, who fought his way to the top commencing with little.

From his youth in Boston to his middle years in Philadelphia, he plied himself ever upward. Often labeled a "money-grubber" by his competitors, he philosophically shook off the insult to cheerfully take away their patrons, as they were trying to take away his.

Still, belied by an outward appearance of avarice during

the early days in his career, he had an inner earnestness to do his fellow man well, which surfaced as his affluence grew. "A rich rogue," he would quote in the first issue of *Poor Richard's Almanack* in 1733, "is like a fat hog, who never does good until dead as a log." Of his final belief in this, we shall observe in the following pages...

"I hope that posterity might know the means by which I achiev'd success; and perhaps find these means suitable in there own situation, and therefore fit to be imitat'd."
Benjamin Franklin
(1706 – 1790)

The Story:
Birth to Retirement

The year was 1706. In England, Queen Anne was the reigning monarch. In the colonies, Cambridge's Harvard College would soon turn seventy; Boston was seventy-five; and a squalling baby boy, named for an uncle Benjamin, was born in a little house on Milk Street [1].

Baby Ben's father, Josiah Franklin, had immigrated to Boston from Branbury in Oxfordshire, England in 1683. Although early apprenticed as a silk dyer, by the time of this son's birth he ran a small candle making and soap boiling shop out of his home. Six years later, the business so prospered he moved family and shop to a new and larger home on the corner of Union and Hanover Streets.

It was here, at the age of 10, that Ben reluctantly joined his father in the business. "Accordingly," he wrote in his autobiography, "I was employ'd in cutting wicks for the candles, filling the dipping-mold and the molds for the cast candles, attending the shop, going on errands, etc... I dis-lik'd the trade."

Ben's mother, Abiah, was born within the island settle-ment of Nantucket, south of Cape Cod on August 15, 1667.

Very little else is known of her personal life, except that she was Josiah's second wife, was the last daughter of Peter and Mary Morrill Folger, two of New England's first set-tlers, and was an ancestor to James Athearn Folger, founder of Folgers Coffee in the 19th century.

It was also recorded that she was "robust and prolific," having "suckled all of her ten children," and was "a discreet and virtuous woman."

Both Josiah and Abiah lived to grow old together, and now lie in Boston's Granary Burying Ground.

The Boston of Ben Franklin's birth and youth was the largest and most important business town in the colonies. Some three hundred merchants had set up shop by 1706. By 1722, the number had tripled. Boston's population had risen to 12,000, its forty-one streets containing a maze of nearly 3,000 buildings, mostly shoddily put together tene-ment houses.

And mansions were constructed to satisfy the require-ment of wealthier merchants.

For young Ben Franklin the seeds for the first half of his adult life were planted. Commerce and exchange were the way to "virtue, wealth, power, and prestige."

Ben assisted his father for two years. But, by the age of 12, his dislike for the business was clearly evident and Josiah, fearing he would soon "head for the adventurous seas" as did another son several years earlier, scrambled to find a suitable occupation for the unhappy lad.

"[My] bookish inclination, at length determined my father to make me a printer, though he had already one son [James] in the profession."

In 1717, James Franklin, having apprenticed as a printer in London, returned home to open his own shop in the heart of Boston's business district. Nine years the boy's senior, he relished the idea of mastering Ben's apprenticeship.

And neither did Ben mind, for a time. He liked the work, if not his brother's tyrannical disposition, and set about learning every measure of it. In disregarding the beatings often dealt him, he knew the trade would make him money if he kept his personal feelings silent.

At the age of 13, he wrote and published two poems: 'The Lighthouse Tragedy,' recounting the recent drowning of a Captain Worthylake [with his wife and two daughters] and 'The Taking of Teach, the Pirate,'a sailor song on the death of Blackbeard. "They were wretched stuff," he admits to us, but his brother loved them and ordered him to hawk the compositions on the streets of Boston. "The first sold wonderfully, the event being recent, having made a great noise. This flatter'd my vanity. But my father discourag'd me, by ridiculing my performances, and telling me verse-makers were generally beggars; so I escap'd being a poet, most probably a bad one."

By 1719, Ben began to feel and act as more a part owner in the business than as an apprentice. He commenced negotiating contracts for, and with, his brother. In that year they secured an agreement to print *The Boston Gazette*, one of that city's two newspapers.

Though losing the contract after only forty issues, James undauntedly decided to prepare the publication of his own sheet, with young Ben positioned as the typesetter. Two years later, on Monday, August 7, 1721 [old style reckoning], *The New-England Courant* would emerge without the blessings of the Franklin family or friends, who had argued the futility of a third Boston newspaper.

The New-England Courant, a weekly journal modeled on London's short-lived [1711-12] sheet called *The Spectator*, consisted of "news" in the form of opinionated letters sent in by various contributors.

Ben, soon tiring of merely setting type for the views of others, wished to express his own opinions and ideas but feared readers would not pay attention to a 16-year-old boy. They would, though, listen to middle-aged Silence Dogood, widow of a country minister.

From April to October of 1722, the fictitious Silence Dogood wrote fourteen letters to *The New-England Courant*.

Encouraged by the success and apparent approval of the letters, Ben excitedly and proudly told his brother he was the writer. But James disapproved, leading to an inevitable relationship split. "Tho' a brother, he considered himself as my master, and me as his apprentice, and accordingly expected the same services from me as he would from another, while I thought he demean'd me too much in some requir'd of me, who from a brother expected more indulgence. Our disputes were often brought before our father, and I fancy I was generally in the right, or perchance a better pleader, because the judgment was generally in my favor. But my brother was passionate and had often beat me, which I took extreamly [sic] amiss; and thinking my apprenticeship very tedious, I was continually wishing for an opportunity to shorten it..."

Meanwhile, the infamous Cotton Mather was supporting smallpox inoculations from his pulpit in answer to the 1721 Boston epidemic introduced from the West Indies. However, the clergyman's role in the Salem witch trials of 1692 had damaged his reputation for enlightenment and his arguments for immunization to fight the dreaded disease were met with scorn. To counter what he felt was mere dissention, he circulated letters to a roster of neighboring doctors in an attempt to bolster his position.

One doctor, Zabdiel Boylston, replied: "...I will try it on my son, Thomas, and my two servants and, if successful, will continue the treatment." The experiment did indeed prove a success, and Dr. Boylston proceeded to vaccinate 241 patients. Of these, six who were beyond help died.

Still, many feared this new treatment, and fear leads to violence. Mather and Boylston were assaulted by a mob on the streets of Boston, followed by a homemade bomb tossed into Mather's study. "This town," thundered the furious Mather, "has become a hell upon earth. Possessed by Satan."

James Franklin, needing a distraction from his rebellious younger brother, took up the fight against inoculation in allowing the *Courant*'s contributors — many of whom were medical students — to voice their ridicule of Mather and his ideas. Mather retaliated by labeling the *Courant* "…a notorious, scandalous paper, …full freighted with nonsense, unmanliness, profaneness, immorality, arrogance, calumnies, lies, contradictions and what-not, all tending to quarrels and diversions, and to debauch and corrupt the minds and manner of New-England." The Rev. Increase Mather further defended his son's stand by adding: "…if the civil authorities do not take action …some awful judgment will come upon the land and the wrath of God will arise and there will be no remedy."[2]

The civil authorities did take action, though not for the reason predicted by the clergyman. James Franklin made the mistake of criticizing the local government for being "casual in dealing with pirates."

On June 11, 1722, the Massachusetts General Court ordered his arrest and the legislature jailed him from June 12th to July 7th.

This opened Ben's bid toward freedom. He took over and ran the newspaper until his brother's release.

Then, in January of 1723, James again offended by penning a *Courant* article charging "Hypocritical pretenders to religion [referring to the Mathers] were worse for a commonwealth than those who were openly profane."

Josiah, attempting a wearied defense of his contentious son, held up his hands in despair when the court issued this order: "James Franklin should no longer print the paper called *The New-England Courant*."

Thinking to thwart the order and please his father, James publicly released Ben from his apprenticeship and placed him in full charge of the paper.

But behind closed doors, he forced the boy to sign a subsequent secret agreement in which Ben was to remain an indentured servant until he reached the age of 21.

Shaking this new vexation off to bide his time, the 17-year-old published the *Courant* successfully for several months until "a fresh difference arising between my brother and me, I took it upon myself to assert my freedom, presuming that he would not venture to produce the new indentures."

James sputtered with anger as he watched his ungrateful apprentice grab his hat and walk out on him. How dare he! This action nullified any brotherly affection he may have once had.

He blackballed Ben from every printer in Boston [3].

Unable to find work and shunned as a fellow tradesman over the following weeks, Ben managed to sell some books "to raise a little money" and secretly sailed for New York aboard the sloop *Speedwell* on September 25th, arriving on Friday, September 27th.

The New York of 1723 was little more than a village on the tip of Manhattan Island. Smaller than Boston, it boasted one printer — William Bradford — who had no work for the young traveler, but suggested he try Philadelphia.

"My son Andrew owns a growing shop there," Bradford offered. "He might be in a position to furnish you with employment."

So Ben, with even less money lining his pockets, sailed again into an unknown destiny.

Although less than a century old, the Quaker city of Philadelphia had almost equaled the population of Boston by the year 1723, with shops of every conceivable variety dotting High Street following recovery of an economic depression. The "City of Brotherly Love" now stood as a haven for men of enterprise.

"Men such as myself," smiled Benjamin Franklin in later life.

That later life was in the year 1748, yet 1723 saw Ben enter Philadelphia as a tattered, tired, hungry boy with one Dutch dollar to his name, munching on a stale roll.

"I made myself as tidy as I could and went to see Andrew Bradford the printer's," recalled Ben. "I found in the shop the old man his father, whom I had met in New York, and who traveling on horseback had got to Philadelphia before me... He introduced me to his son, who receiv'd me civilly, gave me a breakfast, but told me he did not at present want a hand, being lately suppli'd with one. But there was another printer in town lately set up, one Keimer, who perhaps might employ me..."

And so, with a purpose written over his otherwise boyish countenance, Ben set out for Keimer's shop, accompanied by the helpful William Bradford.

Samuel Keimer, eccentric, scholastic in his own mind, and sporting a Mosaic beard, was working on a degenerate old press when Ben and Bradford entered the shop. A smile cracked the old man's craggy face until he learned the younger of the two, merely a boy, was looking for work.

Though arguing that he needed customers, not employees, Keimer hired Ben as a journeyman compositor through

William Bradford's persuasive nature but thought better of it as each payday depleted his coffers a little more.

Nevertheless, Ben was content again.

He was re-establishing himself in the trade he enjoyed, had money in his pockets, and was soon courting pretty, young Deborah Read, the daughter of his landlord.

Better still, he stood notice by no less a personage than the governor of Pennsylvania, Sir William Keith.

Provincial Governor Keith, who had met Ben at Keimer's shop several weeks earlier and was moved by his writing skills and enthusiasm, proposed he return to Boston and ask his father to finance him in his own business. Barring this, he would set the young man up himself, give him exclusive printing for the Pennsylvania colonies and pay for any incidentals needed to keep the business running.

Ben could hardly believe his luck. His own father had refused to resource his ambition when he returned home, yet this virtual stranger now further suggested he send his prospective young ward to London for the purchase of primary equipment. Letters of introduction and credit would be placed in a mail pouch carried aboard ship.

On November 15, 1724, the *London Hope* [4], transporting a jubilant Ben Franklin and a friend, James Ralph, embarked for England. Even the ship's name seemed to bear good tidings.

Thirty-nine days later, the ship's passengers were disembarking and Ben was anxiously looking for the letters. None were found addressed to his care.

Sadly pulling up a crate and sitting, he realized a truth.

Sir William Keith, provincial governor of Pennsylvania and friend to all, was a dreamer. He "wished to please everybody and, having little to give, he gave them expectations."

Ben walked the streets of London, broke and alone once more in a strange city. It was Christmas Eve, he was eighteen-years-old, and he wanted to go home — to America — but lacked even the fare for passage.

His vow was to never let it happen again.

But that was a pledge for the future.

This day, inevitable panic tore at his insides. He still had 20 guineas, enough for a few days' food and lodging if he were careful in his spending, but could he survive for long in this eminent city? A dark cloud seemed to chill him.

Tagging merrily beside him, James Ralph suggested they search out Thomas Denham, a Quaker merchant they had met and befriended on the voyage over, and ask his advice.

Nineteen-year-old James Ralph fancied himself a poet and left his family in pursuit of this illusion. Unknown to Ben at that time, he intended to return neither to Philadelphia, nor to his wife and child.

Thomas Denham readily advised Ben to: "Endeavor getting some employment in the way of my business. 'Among the printers here,' said he, 'you will improve yourself, and when you return to America, you will set up to greater advantage.' "

Ben took the advice and was soon working for Samuel Palmer's. London's foremost printing house.

Again he was making money but, as is the want of a teenage boy, was not saving it. With James Ralph, who was still out of work and living with him, he spent "a good deal of my earnings in going to plays and other places of amusement... In fact, by our expenses, I was constantly kept unable to pay my passage [home]."

Interestingly, and luckily for Ben, within a year their friendship "had a parting of the ways" over Ralph's new mistress.

As the story goes: It seems Ralph cultivated a relationship with a young woman and her little girl and moved in with them. Since he still had no prospect for employment in London, and her income was not sufficient to support all, he took a position as a schoolmaster in the village of Berkshire, England. In a letter to Ben, he asked that his friend take charge of the woman until his return. "Mrs. T____ [the mistress], having on his account lost her friends and business, was often in distresses, and us'd to send for me, and borrow what I could spare to help her out of them. I grew fond of her company, and being at that time under no religious retraint, and presuming upon my importance to her, I attempted familiarities (another erratum [5]), which she repuls'd with a proper resentment, and acquaint'd him with my behavior. This made a breach between us; and, when he returned again to London, he let me know he thought I had cancel'd all the obligations he had been under to me. So I found that I was never to expect his repaying me what I had lent him, or advanc'd for him. This, however, was not then of much consequence, as he was totally unable; and in the loss of his friendship, I found myself reliev'd of a burden.

"I now began to think of getting a little money up-front, and expecting better work I left Palmer's to work at Watts', near Lincoln Inn Fields, a still greater printing-house. Here I continued all the rest of my stay in London."

Throughout his eighteen months in London, Ben had often paid visits to Thomas Denham and now the merchant, having concluded his business, was preparing for a return to Philadelphia.

Thomas Denham, having failed in his Bristol, England mercantile establishment, fled to America to escape ever increasing debts and re-establish himself. Over the years, he regained his fortune and returned to England, where he repaid all creditors with interest.

Now Ben, watching his good friend pack his bags for the trip home, regretted his leaving and implored him to stay. Denham shook his head, smiled, and explained why this was not possible but had something in mind, which might keep the two together if his companion was in agreement.

He had plans for a new store. Would Ben be interested in returning to Philadelphia as his clerk at £50 per year? Would he be opposed to giving up the printing business? Would he accept an advance of £10 for his passage?

Ben sat back to look at his friend for several minutes as he weighed the pros and cons of this fresh proposition.

The pros were: [1] Mr. Denham was a doer, not a talker. [2] Unlike Governor Keith, Mr. Denham had the money to accomplish his plans. [3] He would go home at last.

He reflected on only one con: He would be giving up a trade in which he knew nearly everything for one in which he knew absolutely nothing.

He returned his thoughts to another pro: Almost every merchant he had come into contact, stemming from his days in Boston, were wealthy.

The pros won out. He could learn merchandising.

On July 23, 1726, a ship left the docks of Newcastle, England. Among the twenty-five passengers waving farewell at the rail stood Benjamin Franklin and Thomas Denham. Its hold contained abundant supplies for a new store.

During the quiet voyage home, Ben would sit and rest his back against a cabin wall to write a journal, formulating within its pages a plan for regulating his future conduct in life.

Unfortunately, most of the manuscript has been lost to time, with only the first four points having survived. They are, even so, very important points:

1. **It is necessary for me to be extremely frugal for some time, until I have paid what I owe.**

2. **To endeavor to speak truth in every instance; to give nobody expectations that are not likely to be answered, but aim at sincerity in every word and action.**

3. **To apply myself industriously in every business I take in hand, and not divert my mind from my business by any ill-judged project of suddenly growing rich; for industry and patience are the**

surest means to plenty.

4. **I resolve to speak ill of no man what-**
ever, not even in a matter of truth;
but rather by some means excuse the
faults I hear charged upon others, and
upon proper occasions speak all the
good I know of everybody. [6]

When Ben arrived in his beloved Philadelphia on Oct-ober 11, 1726, he wasted no time in scouting the city and looking up old friends. He was, though, reluctant to resume his courtship with Deborah Read, since he had written her no more than one letter during his time abroad; and that to say he was "not likely soon to return."

Deborah Read, despairing of ever seeing Ben again, had been persuaded by her mother and friends to marry an ap-parently successful potter named John Rogers.

But Rogers was a somewhat shiftless character, paying little attention to business and even much less to Deborah. When she discovered he had another wife, abandoned somewhere in England, she left him and moved back to the secluded safety of her mother's house. [7]

Ben slowly walked up the steps to the house he had call-ed home almost two years earlier. Placing a hesitant hand upon the knocker, he was about to turn away when a sad-eyed young woman opened the door. He looked at her with sorrow and guilt. Had he the capacity for tears, they would have flowed not only from his eyes but also from his heart.

Although an unlawful public display, he reached out and

and took her into his arms. And she cried.

In the meantime, Thomas Denham had been busy.

A small building was rented on Water St.; supplies were brought in, inventoried and placed on racks and shelves; and a crude "Open for Business" sign was fashioned and placed in a front window.

Ben, having been given extra time to reacquaint himself with his friends, now returned with several in tow as prospective customers. The older man's face lit up as the cashbox rang happily to the sound of coins.

"I attended the business diligently," Ben tells us, "studied accounts, and grew, in a little time, expert at selling. We lodg'd and boarded together; he counsel'd me as a father, having a sincere regard for me. I respect'd and loved him, and we might have gone on together very happy..."

But unforeseeable death would part the two in 1728, and Ben would re-enter the printing business. "I forget what his distemper was; it held him a long time, and at length carried him off. He left me a small legacy in a nuncupative will, as a token of kindness for me, and he left me once more to the wide world, for the store was taken into the care of his executors, and my employment under him ended."

Samuel Keimer's printing business had expanded with the city's rapid growth during Ben's absence and now, hearing of his former employee's latest plight, gleefully offered to take him back as his foreman. The pretentious young Franklin was a failure. And Keimer was enjoying every morsel of it.

Yet, behind the satisfaction of seeing the young man's debasement, the roguish Keimer actually needed Ben. Of the several employees he now had, none had been "bred to the business; nor were they any good." Franklin, he knew, would "instruct them properly" and "put his printing-house in order." After that, who knows? Such was in the mind of Samuel Keimer.

Having little trust for the old schemer, Ben put off accepting the position until he found his new trade of merchandising unavailable to newcomers. "I tri'd for further employment as a merchant's clerk; but not readily meeting with any, I closed again with Keimer."

Ben's apprehensions proved correct. Within six months — when the employees were well trained and the shop put in order — he was fired through a concocted argument by the old man.

Though Keimer offered him three months' notice, Ben's boyish ego held him as it had in Boston. He put on his hat and tramped toward the door, asking a sympathetic Hugh Meredith to fetch his things to his lodgings.

When a jobless Ben Franklin walked out of Samuel Keimer's shop, he was nearly broke. Over the past months he had saved barely enough money to live on for the next few days. This time he was even more frightened than he had been in London.

During the four years since leaving home, he had met with nothing but failure. Perhaps it would be best to return and take up his father's trade. Why go on struggling here, when Boston and family would surely welcome him back.

If he humbled himself enough.

Late that evening a slow rap on his door startled Ben's thoughts to the present and was opened to a tilting Hugh Meredith; a box, containing his friend's belongings, held loosely under one arm. Meredith swayed to the left, then to the right, as Ben extended a hand...

Thirty-year-old Hugh Meredith was a Welsh Pennsylvania farmer who had come to Philadelphia in the hope of quenching his thirst for wealth.

Instead, he found stingy old Samuel Keimer, paying just enough money for daily food and lodging and nights in taverns, where he drank away his sorrows.

In the months spent under Ben's guidance, he grew to like and respect the younger man and began to work harder and drink less. But he could never quite release himself from the mind-numbing liquid, absorbing heavily in times of grief. This was one of those times...

...Meredith took the proffered hand, more as a balance than a greeting, and dropped to the nearest chair, where he sobered to a small extent as Ben told of his decision to return to Boston.

Shaking his head to clear a fog, Meredith related a tale of Keimer's troubles. The old skinflint was largely in debt, owing more than he was worth, and was headed for bankrupcy.

If Ben would stay here, pushed Meredith, Keimer's problems will necessitate another printer in Philadelphia.

Ben countered with an argument of not having any money, pointing out that everything he tries ends in failure. He was tired of starting over with no degree of success and wished he had died when a pleurisy struck him six months earlier [8]. "A life without some measure of success is no life at all," he lamented.

Meredith, nearly sobered now, responded by offering an arrangement he conceived might alter the course of his pensive friend's life.

His father, he felt sure, would put up the money if he and Ben went into partnership.

"I'm no printer," admitted Meredith, "but if you furnish the skill, and I the stock, we'll share equally."

Ben liked the idea and immediately agreed. If this venture did not work out, he perhaps thought, at least he gave it another try. Besides, to confront his father and brother James under such impoverished circumstances would crush whatever was left of his fragile spirit.

Here, we should take a quick look into Benjamin Franklin's character up to this stage in his life:

By the age of twenty-one, he had not put into action the four points of the plan he had written during his voyage back to America in 1726.

Although his autobiography states, "Perhaps the most important part of that journal is the plan to be found in it, which I form'd at sea, regulating my future conduct in life. It is the more remarkable, as being form'd when I was so young, and yet being pretty faithfully adhered to quite thro' to old age,"

we must beg to differ.

Whether he followed whatever additional directives, at this time or later, we may never know. However, an analysis of the points he would consider most important — having numbered them first — shows a digression from his well-meant intentions:

1. Ben spent as much money as he made, saving a modicum. Those, to which he had owed for several years, including Boston's Dr. Boylston and a neighbor named Vernon, were still waiting.

2. Notwithstanding a fundamental integrity, at this age he still stretched the truth when faced with an awkward situation. As when Deborah Read asked him if he had "seen other women" during his stay in London.

   What about giving expectations? As with Governor Keith he had no means of fulfillment, so offered none at this phase in his life. But as the years went on, and he grew in maturity and prosperity, one could expect all promises by Benjamin Franklin kept.

3. From early on, Ben Franklin was industrious. However, he lacked the patience his plan called for. This shortcoming caused his youthful failures. In his attempts to grow suddenly rich,

he plowed into every opportunity without study.

Had he checked the nature of Governor Keith before traveling to London, he would have avoided his first bit of woe. True, this probably induced him to eventually write the plan, but it did not prevent his making the same impatient mistake later. Notably, when Keimer offered to allow him to manage his business. At "substantially high pay," we might add. He could have broached the steadfast Andrew Bradford at lower wages, since Bradford was now interested in Ben's work and was willing to hire him.

4. Ben Franklin had a temper throughout his life, before and after the plan.

In arguments with his older brother James, James Ralph, Samuel Keimer and later Hugh Meredith, he would vent his wrath verbally. To those who aroused his anger from a distance, he lashed out through the printed word.

As he grew older, less insecure and wiser he would remain quiet if angered, or attempt to ease an unpleasant conversation with a joke. If both failed, he would shrug his broad shoulders and turn from his antagonist. In

this, he found himself the victor. For his opponent's rage increased to an extensive shade of purple, with no one mentally available to allow for its escape.

His writings, too, mellowed with age.

And he did, indeed, learn to speak ill of no man. Though some of his fellow Founding Fathers — John Adams for one — seldom returned the compliment.

Within three days of Hugh Meredith's shaky exit, Ben prepared to meet the elder Meredith.

After bathing, toweling and combing out his long brown hair, he studied himself in his full-length looking glass.

Standing about 5′ 10″, he had the barrel-build of a bear. His face was not handsome, yet the large gray eyes, topped with a penetrating gaze, made it compelling. The wide mouth, corners turned toward a shrewd smile, completed the picture.

He shrugged, neither liking nor disliking the reflection, and dressed into refreshingly clean cloths. Donning his tricorn, he sat on the edge of his bed to await the arrival of Hugh Meredith.

When Meredith rapped on the door fifteen minutes later, both young men went off to what they hoped would be a fresh beginning.

The elder Meredith greeted and liked Ben from the outset. What he had heard of his son's friend was impressive, but the cleanly dressed person standing before him impressed him even more. That, coupled with Ben's abatement of his son's drinking, made a financial arrangement inevitable.

Sitting for the first time since arriving, Ben made a list of equipment to order from London.

"While awaiting the shipment," Ben suggested, "Hugh will finish his apprenticeship with Keimer. I will spend my time in leisure until our new business can be set in motion,"

Or so he thought…

Samuel Keimer was in a frenzy.

New Jersey was offering a large order for printing their paper money and he had just fired the only man in the colonies able to do the job.

Fearing Andrew Bradford would secure the order by hiring Ben, he appeared at his former employee's door with a smile of contrition.

With hat in hand, Keimer admonished himself for allowing "such a trifling misunderstanding to come between old friends."   If Ben will find himself agreeable for a return to work, at 'twice the salary you were receiving before our unfortunate incident," he would have full control of the business.

Ben knew of New Jersey's offer and enjoyed watching the old fool squirm. At length, he told Keimer he would think about it, bidding him "good-morrow."

He then went directly to the Merediths, excitedly reporting his visit from Keimer. Hugh urged him to accept the position, praying his need for extra training under Ben. Too, the additional income would serve in preparations for their new shop.

Within a week, Ben and Keimer were off to Burlington, New Jersey.

Keimer was as nervous as a mouse cornered by a cat. If this trip came to naught, he was ruined. His future depended on the big man sitting relaxed beside him.

They were greeted by a delegation of public officials as their carriage arrived, and the job was soon theirs. Ben had supplied the conversation and figures during the interview; while Keimer remained out of the way, feverishly stroking his beard.

So struck were the officiates with this enterprising young printer, he was summoned to their homes and "intoduc'd round." Keimer was all but ignored. But what did he care? He was to get a large sum of money, while his ostentatious employee could bask only in the glory of the moment.

Little did the old man realize in his self-absorbed reasoning, that that "moment" assured his employee a lifetime of valuable contacts?

When the two returned to Philadelphia, Ben constructed America's first copperplate press and proceeded to cut the ornaments for the bills.

Keimer, again in control of his world, strut his shop with arms folded across a haughty chest.

Occasionally, he would unfold the limbs and briskly rub his hands together, but not because he was cold. This printing job would furnish him with enough profit to keep him going for a year or more.

Springtime came and, with it, the new equipment from London.

Like a released schoolboy, 22-year-old Ben ran for the docks, followed on his heels by an equally exuberant Hugh Meredith. Both checked the manifest and gave directions for delivery, blundering their words to such a caliber as to completely confuse the draymen.

Laughter could be heard all the way to the new shop.

For young Benjamin Franklin, the dark clouds were lifting. Shadows of the past were giving way to a light in the future.

When the press and types were readied, a sign was hoisted above the shop's door by the two proud young men.

It read simply:

FRANKLIN and MEREDITH, printers

The knavish Keimer was seething. When Franklin and Meredith left his employ, in what he thought was a congenial departure, they said nothing of starting a new printing-house. How dare they trick him like this! He must do something to put the young upstarts out of business.

FRANKLIN and MEREDITH located itself near the Philadelphia Market on High Street [now Market Street]. The rent was £24 a year, but by subletting rooms to a Junto [9] member and his family the burden was eased.

From its beginning the new business prospered. The day it opened brought a patron paying five shillings. The elder Meredith sent associates who needed bills printed. Andrew

Bradford, too, presented them with customers he was unable to handle.

But one day, while Ben bustled about behind the counter, an old raven entered. His name was Samuel Mickle, a self-appointed foreteller of evil tidings known in the early centuries as "a croaker."

Looking around the shop while shaking his head sadly, Mickle informed a smiling Ben that his business could not possibly succeed. Philadelphia's boom was over, he said.

Numbering the recent failures on his fingers, he stressed there was nothing to look forward to but ruin and desolation.

As a frown replaced Ben's smile, Mickle left the shop, satisfied he had brought misery to yet another life.

Several days passed before Ben was able to forget Samuel Mickle. The elder was a prominent citizen. Perhaps he knew of what he spoke. Had the two met prior to the business being set up, he mused, he most likely would have backed out of the venture.

But it was too late now he reflectively shook his head. There was too much at stake. He could not fail again!

Meanwhile, Ben's Junto members were also exerting all effort to help him succeed. Friends, and friends of friends, were sent to the shop.

FRANKLIN and MEREDITH soon obtained a contract to print forty pages of a huge folio entitled: *Historie of the Rise, Increase, and Progress of the Christian People called Quakers.* Keimer was to print the rest.

Hugh worked the press, while Ben set the type.

Ben's aim was to set one page a day, often working far into the night. Once, when he accidentally jumbled a tray of type, he reset everything before going to bed.

This quality of "industry" was soon noticed by the people of Philadelphia. Even old Mickle mumbled, "Franklin might do something with his business."

One member of the Merchant's Every-night Club, which comprised the city's most respected businessmen, attested seeing... "Franklin at work when members leave for home at night, and again the next morning before most of us are abroad."

Along with further business came George Webb, a former co-worker at Keimer's, looking for a position as a journeyman.

Or so he said.

Ben liked George and regretted having to turn his friend away, but suggested he try again later. He had plans for the start of a newspaper.

The only newspaper south of New England was Andrew Bradford's *American Weekly Mercury*, a dull reading, and mismanaged, sad affair. Ben hoped to produce a paper to move the people and city he loved to mirth and laughter.

Ben's secret was quickly brought to Keimer, who knew what to do. He had the immediate money and, from what George Webb had told him, **FRANKLIN and MEREDITH** would not have the means to initiate its paper for several months. Perfect!

On December 24, 1728, just weeks of sending Webb to the new print shop,Keimer pulled the first issue of his newspaper off the press. A self-satisfied smile etched his face as he read its title: *The Universal Instructor in All Arts and Sciences, and the Pennsylvania Gazette.* Subscriptions: ten shillings a year. Advertisers were to pay three shillings each to hawk their wares.

Keimer was preparing to retire a wealthy man.

Forestalled by Keimer, Ben grabbed his pen and contributed a series of satirical articles to the *Weekly Mercury*, signed merrily the "Busy-Body."

Basically a continuation of the "Silence Dogood" letters of his teen years, the "Busy-Body" papers brought in a flow of new subscribers to the *Weekly Mercury*.

The years had engendered a marked change to his writing style, however. Whereas the "Dogood" letters were seriously provocative, the "Busy-Body" papers were humorously whimsical. Gone was his anger at everyone as he wrote. His passion was focused on one person, Samuel Keimer; to the delight of readers who refused to pass a week without deliciously ingesting the latest installment.

Keimer knew the "Busy-Body" papers were trained toward him alone and attempted publishing counterattacks. But they were too feeble to do any good. He was losing ground, as well as subscribers and advertisers.

Finally, at the end of August 1729, heavily in debt and wishing to flee the colonies, he threw up his hands in defeat and sold his paper unknowingly to the "Busy-Body" himself [10].

FRANKLIN and MEREDITH now owned a newspaper. Ben dropped most of its pompous title and renamed it simply the *Pennsylvania Gazette*.

Originally the paper, under Keimer, consisted of columns reprinted from "Chamber's Dictionary of the Arts and Sciences." Fillers were news tidbits and political addresses.

Ben considered the reprinting of a dictionary not in the best interest of conveying knowledge, so set about an editorial change.

To readers of the first issue of his *Gazette*, dated Thursday, September 25 to Thursday, October 2, 1729, he wrote:

> **We ask assistance, because we are fully sensible, that to publish a good newspaper is not so easy an undertaking as many people imagine it to be. The author of a Gazette (in the opinion of the learned) ought to be qualified with an extensive acquaintance with languages, a great easiness and command of writing, and relating things clearly and intelligently, and in a few words; he should be able to speak to men both by land and sea; be well acquaint'd with geography, with the historie of time, with the secret interests of princes and states; the secrets of courts, and the manners and customs of all nations. Men thus accomplished are very rare in this remote part of the world; and it would be well if the writer of these papers could make up among his friends what he lacks himself. Upon the whole, we may assure the publick that, as far as every encouragement we meet**

will enable us, no care or pains, shall be disregard'd that may make the Pennsylvania Gazette as agreeable and useful an enjoyment as the nature of the thing can be.

Taking his cue from experiences as James' apprentice, Ben was asking for contributors to the new paper. Reader participation meant reader enjoyment. And reader enjoyment meant more subscribers. It was as simple as that.

The paper flourished.

Andrew Bradford was now **FRANKLIN and MEREDITH**'s only competitor in Philadelphia.

Although the *Weekly Mercury* was virtually a thing of the past, Bradford still printed public documents for Pennsylvania. But his work, though considered acceptable, was rather sloppy to the average observer and Ben, glancing at one of the documents, shook his head.

Taking it back to his shop, he reprinted it "elegantly and correctly" and sent a copy to each member of the Assembly. As a result, and with the help of Andrew Hamilton, a lawyer he had met aboard the *London Hope* in 1724, **FRANKLIN and MEREDITH** was chosen official printers for the Pennsylvania colonies; the position promised five years earlier by Provincial Governor Keith.

Human nature seems to mandate that we relax during periods of prosperity. So it was with Ben Franklin. Money flowed in and, as quickly, poured out. When the ingress of currency slowed for a time, new furnishings were bought on credit. And, though the original equipment purchased from

London still claimed a balance of £100, there was no worry. The elder Meredith had promised to make good on the bill.

Unfortunately, another bubble burst in Ben's budding career. The elder Meredith went bankrupt and found himself unable to meet the obligation. As a result, the merchant for the London firm threatened a lawsuit to repossess the equipment and foreclose on the enterprise.

FRANKLIN and MEREDITH was in trouble. There was no way to raise that kind of money. The partners talked, argued, and finally reached an agreement. Hugh, wishing to leave Philadelphia and its growing iniquities far behind and join the Welsh farm settlements of North Carolina, wanted out.

His offer was to sell out to Ben with the following stipulations: 1. Ben would take charge of his business and personal debts. 2. Repay the money already advanced by his father. 3. Provide him personally with £30 and a saddle.

Considering Hugh had been drinking heavily for several months, exhibiting himself more as a liability than an asset, Ben felt it better to be rid of him and willingly agreed to these terms.

Still, he had no money. How or where could he raise it?

Here, Ben's forming of the Junto in 1727 was to pay off in 1729.

Wealthy member Robert Grace and merchant's clerk member William Coleman approached him separately with a proposal to advance whatever monies deemed necessary to get him out of his dire straits, provided the drunken Hugh Meredith leave the partnership.

Since the unfortunate partnership had already been dissolved in Ben's eyes, he accepted half the money offered from each and, with cash in hand, settled the Merediths, the merchant for the London firm and the long-standing arrears to Dr. Boylston and Vernon.

And so, at the age of twenty-four, a young Benjamin Franklin stood proudly as the sole owner of his own printing business.

Ben was sole owner of **B. FRANKLIN** in name only; he was soon to caution himself, for he still had the outstanding loans advanced by Grace and Coleman to repay.

This, coupled with the nagging fear of another failure, brought nights awakened in cold sweats.

Suppose Grace and Coleman were to renege on their contract to allow for a three-year return period on the loans, and seized the business?

They would have to be repaid as soon as possible.

In order to accomplish this, he would need to present himself as a model businessman at all times. The citizens would again know of his industry.

"In order to secure my credit and character as a tradesman, I took care not only to be **really** industrious and frugal, but to avoid all appearances to the contrary. I drest plainly; I was seen at no places of idle diversion. I never went a-fishing and shooting..."

His tactics proved effective.

"Thus being esteem'd an industrious, thriving young man and paying only for what I bought, the merchants who imported stationery solicited my custom..."

With the opening of a stationery section coinciding with the success of his *Gazette*, and still commissioned the printer for Pennsylvania, business improved sufficiently to allow for recompensing Grace and Coleman's debts within the allotted time.

Ben need never have feared Robert Grace and William Coleman. Records show they did not intend to shatter their friend's dreams.

Ben Franklin was bent on success. Samuel Keimer's last apprentice, David Harry, tried a competing print shop for a time, but eventually followed his master to Barbados.

Of his remaining Philadelphia rivals, Andrew Bradford now ran a post office and was losing interest in printing. Even so, he attempted to prevent his post riders from delivering Ben's *Gazette*. An action defeated, to a comical conclusion, by Ben secretly bribing the riders.

On September 1, 1730, Ben Franklin married his long-suffering sweetheart, Deborah Read Rogers, in what could be considered a civil ceremony.

No record to substantiate any marriage has ever been established, however, and some question as to its legitimacy has plagued Franklin historians for over two centuries. But this is best left for others to decide, or to scratch their heads over. For us, it is sufficient to accept Deborah as Mrs. Benjamin Franklin in the eyes of the world in which she lived. And, although Ben is reported to have had affairs throughout his marriage, she was always his "dear Debbie" or "My dear child" until her passing forty-four years later.

The Entrepreneurial Ben Franklin

A big, buxom woman, Deborah Franklin was a tempestuous wife at times. Yet Ben never seemed to mind. "Better a high-spirited woman," he would say, "than a weak and whining one." Once, when a friend remarked of her turbulent temper toward her newly found husband, he answered: "Don't you know that all wives are right!"

In contrast to her outbursts — reported to have taken place before and after their union — Deborah Franklin profoundly loved Ben, or "pappy" as she affectionately called him. This love proved itself within just ten months of their joining together.

Historical documents record Ben's early life as "given to low women..." Whether from one of these women or, as rumored by his later political enemies, from a maidservant named Barbara, a six-month-old infant was placed in Debbie's arms with no answers given her astonished gasp. Ben simply said, "His name is William."

Ben pampered William from the moment of acceptance into his circle. Either from guilt for having burdened Debbie with an illegitimate offspring, or from inadequacies in his own childhood, he took full charge of the boy; lavishing him with money, gifts, and an education he lacked. Where he skipped meals to buy books, William ate well and purchased whatever he needed or wanted. Where he swam in the waters around Boston for his athletic pleasures, William rode the streets of Philadelphia on a magnificent steed gifted by a doting father. And where his formal education consisted of a meager two years, William attended the finest schools, learned the gentleman's art of Latin, the mysteries of astronomy, and the political sciences of the day.

Nothing was too good for his son; nothing he could not, nor would not, give him.

In 1752, father and son awaited the coming of a thunderstorm. Ben was 46. William, 21.

For weeks everything had been in preparation. A kite, made from a large silk handkerchief and topped with a pointed metal wire, was carried out in readiness. The early afternoon June sky was darkening. Scattered rain began to fall. William grabbed the kite. Ben took hold of a Leyden jar inserted with a metal rod, placed a brass house key in his pocket, and both ran out to a neighboring grazing field like two lads on a romp.

A famous Currier and Ives print depicts Franklin, with a small boy leaping for joy when lightning strikes the kite and shimmers down the string to a key held just inches from the expectant hand of the string-holder.

Nothing could be further from the true facts. Had the lightning struck as portrayed, Ben would have been surely electrocuted. The experiment was dangerous. He knew this and took precautions. Twice, in past laboratory tests, he had been knocked into unconsciousness producing man-made electrical sparks. Nature's lightning, he knew, was a force more powerful than any a man could develop.

The kite was fashioned specifically for the experiment. Its silk handkerchief had a purpose, as this weave is a non-conductor of electricity. The pointed wire topping the kite was devised to ward off an electrical overcharge. A silk ribbon would attach to the kite's string, with the house key attached to the ribbon.

Within minutes of entering the grazing field, the kite was flying high. William flew the kite, while Ben watched from concealment in a small shed nearby. William looked silly flying a kite in the rain but Ben, as one of Philadelphia's leading citizens, would have been reported imbecile should anyone have spotted him prancing through the rainy pasture. "T'was better to wait for the coming deluge to obscure vision."

Lightning could be seen in the distance. Thunder roared. The deluge came. Ben ran out to William, quickly fastened the ribbon and key, and took hold of the string. The kite was now a dot dancing in the beclouded sky.

The storm's fury increased. Lightning flashed ominously. Thunder reverberated throughout the city. Citizens shuttered windows and prayed the menacing bolts would not strike their houses.

Ben, in contrast, hoped his little kite would experience the force of lightning the way he had it planned. Yet, nothing was happening. The little key, which was to conduct the electricity, was still cold to the touch.

Sure an electrical charge would have heated it by now, he directed a knuckle to it several times without any reaction.

Where did he go wrong? Was his hypothesis in error? Was there not enough electricity from lightning after all? Crestfallen, he turned to William and shook his head.

By now the sky was completely black. William, fearing he would catch his death, prepared to leave. Ben stood staring into the murky void; his mind racing through hundreds of past experiments. He had already written *Experiments and Observations on Electricity, Made at Philadelphia in America.*

The scientific world even now debated accepting his discoveries. Would he have to apologies and yield to humiliation?

Then his eyes fell upon the string he held in his hand. The loose strands were standing on end, suspended by what appeared an electrical charge. Triumphantly, he clapped William on the back and pointed. Cautiously moving his knuckle toward the key a familiar tingling went up his arm as flesh touched metal. Bending to retrieve the dropped Leyden jar, which he had thrown to the ground in anger, he directed the key to its protruding rod. Electricity poured easily into the jar.

William, hardly small at a little over six feet in height, leaped with the excitement of their discovery. His father was right. Electricity and heaven's flashing bolts were one and the same.

Unknown to Ben on that stormy day, French scientists successfully conducted the same test in May with an array of elaborate equipment, vindicating his theory. But the "little kite experiment," owing to the possibility of a deadly consequence, would outstrip all other trials.

In September, America's first lightning rod was placed atop the roof of Benjamin Franklin's home on the southeast corner of Race and Second Streets, Philadelphia. William climbed the roof.

In the year 1752, father and son had never been closer.

Yet time, wrote the philosopher, has a way of changing all things.

As the years passed William, always at odds with Debbie, began pulling entirely away from the family unit. Their belief in "a free and separate country" clashed with his own belief in a loyalty to England, leading to a twenty-two year rift between the son and a bitterly hurt father.

In 1762, William, while in England, was appointed royal governor of New Jersey by George III and would, upon returning to America in 1763 continue his loyalist activities throughout the revolution. "I have lost my son," exclaimed a distraught Benjamin Franklin in 1776.

In 1788, though they had partially reconciled four years earlier, Ben wrote in his will: "The part he [William] acted against me in the late war, which is of public notoriety, will account for my leaving him no more of an estate he endeavor'd to deprive me of." In other words, he left him nothing. A decisive reproof to a son he had once cherished.

William died in England of influenza on November 17, 1813, a despondent old man of 82. His first wife, Elizabeth Downes, had died in 1777 of "accumulated distresses" and, with his second wife Mary D'evelin having died following a long illness, his granddaughter Ellen, clasping his hand to her tear-streaked cheek, was the only one near to ease his lonely passing.

In 1731, Ben took a short hiatus from business to found the first circulating library in America. Debbie ran the shop in his absence.

He was now set on firm financial footing and felt a need

to pay back. What better way than expending his "love for books" to a Philadelphia lacking their access?

Still, in his knowing people as they are, he recognized "…that if I were to present such a project as my own, jealousy would swiftly lay it low." Therefore, he cunningly offered himself as an agent for "lovers of reading" and described his plan as "a scheme of a number of friends."

It worked.

An "Articles of Agreement" document was drawn up for the formation of a library on July 1, 1731.

The year 1731 moved on to '32. George Washington was born on Pope's Creek Estate in Westmoreland County, Virginia; George II was king of England; the first colony in Georgia was settling. Philadelphia was breaking ground for its State House, later known as Independence Hall; Deborah Franklin gave birth to a son, Francis Folger Franklin; and **B. FRANKLIN** was preparing to launch *Poor Richard's Almanack*.

At the age of twenty-six, Ben's sights were fully aimed toward the public good. Of *Poor Richard's Almanack*, he wrote: "I considered it a proper vehicle for conveying instruction among the common people, who bought scarcely any other books; I therefore filled all the little spaces that occur'd between the remarkable days in the calendar with proverbial sentences, chiefly such as inculcat'd industry and frugality, as the means of procuring wealth, and thereby securing virtue; it being more difficult for a man in want, to act always honestly, as, to use here one of those proverbs, 'it is hard for an empty sack to stand upright'."

The first advertisement for *Poor Richard's* was published in the *Pennsylvania Gazette* on December 19, 1732: "Just published, for 1733, an almanack, containing the Luminations, Eclipses, Planets' Motions and Aspects, Weather, Sun and Moon's Rising and Setting, High Water, etc.; besides many pleasant and witty Verses, Jests, and Sayings: ... By Richard Saunders, Philomat. Printed and sold by B. FRANKLIN."

Preferring to remain anonymous, Ben adopted Richard Saunders as his pseudonym. Thereupon, whatever wit, wisdom and humor appearing in the almanac came from the amply knowledgeable pen of Poor Richard himself.

In candor, we cannot give Ben credit for creating either Richard Saunders or Poor Richard. Richard Saunders was a 17th century English astrologer/physician, compiler of the *Apollo Anglicanus*; while Poor Richard derived from *Poor Robin*, an almanac published by James Franklin from his new shop in Newport, Rhode Island. Nor can he be accepted as the originator of the many witticisms ascribed him, through Poor Richard, during the almanac's twenty-five years in circulation.

Nevertheless, we must give Ben his due. His innovative approach to *Poor Richard's Almanack* added appeal to the somewhat stodgy almanacs of the day. Readers looked forward to its yearly issue and, by 1748, Poor Richard had become an institution. That year ten thousand copies were sold, with the same number sold yearly until it ceased publication in 1758. It was the most popular reading material in the colonies, second only to the Bible.

Ben, in fashioning the character of Poor Richard, had assumed its identity. As with Silence Dogood he wanted to speak out, yet again feared the public would not listen to him in his own person. Silence Dogood was silenced forever. Poor Richard was not.

As Poor Richard he pretended at astrology, yet made fun of superstition. He pretended to be old and wise, packing his almanac with wisdom of the ages. He spoke of prudence, industry and frugality. He wrote as a moralist admonishing mankind for its lack of order, while upholding for mankind to succeed depended upon men looking out for themselves; that men should work to be happy, and save to be secure. "Industry and frugality," he would bottom many of his articles, "are the natural roads to freedom."

Although Poor Richard took his wit and wisdom from such notables as John Dryden, Alexander Pope, Thomas Fuller, Jonathan Swift, Francis Bacon, Francois Rabelais, Francois de La Rochefoucauld and many others, Ben did not copy their compositions. Instead, he reworked them to suit his purpose and that of his readers. Writing, he contended, should be "smooth, clear, and short." In 1732, Thomas Fuller had written: "It is better to have a hen tomorrow than a egg to-day." Ben revamped it in 1744 to read: "A hen to-day is better than an egg to-morrow."

In 1742, he had laughingly reworked a somewhat obsolete verse to poke fun at himself:

Ben beats his pate and fancies wit will come.
But he may knock, there's nobody home.

Some sage advise which made Poor Richard famous in his day, and Benjamin Franklin remembered today, were published between 1733 and 1758:

Forewarn'd, forearm'd.

Diligence is the mother of good-luck.

Keep thy shop, and thy shop will keep thee.

Necessity never made a good bargain.

There are three faithful friends; an old wife, an old dog, and ready money.

Let thy discontent be thy secret.

Keep your eyes wide open before marriage, half-shut afterwards.

A learned blockhead is a greater blockhead than an ignorant one.

What one relishes, nourishes.

Eat to please thyself, but dress to please others.

He that falls in love with himself, will have no rivals.

Money and good manners make the gentleman.

When the well's dry, we know the worth of water.

Lost time is never found again.

There are three things extremely hard; steel, a diamond, and to know one's self.

Discontent'd minds, and fevers of the body are not cur'd by changing beds or business-es.

If you have no honey in your pot, have some in your mouth.

If you'd know the value of money, go and borrow some.

Work as if you were to live 100 years; pray as if you were to die to-morrow.

The way to be safe, is not to be secure.

When you're an anvil, hold your still; when you're a hammer, strike your fill.

Ben was not the only famous thinker to transcend max-ims, however. In 1750, Poor Richard wrote: "You may be too cunning for one, but not for all." Nearly 113 years later, Abraham Lincoln gave us his own revision: "You may fool all of the people some of the time; you can fool some of the people all of the time; but you can't fool all of the people all the time."

Poor Richard had a tremendous impact on the lives of aspiring Americans in the 18th century. It was a century of hope, and of opportunity for the economically oppressed. Its people sought in *Poor Richard's* examples and proverbs the formula for success. They embraced those observations that emphasized diligence, perseverance, frugality and thrift.

Yet, as the 18th turned into the 19th and 20th centuries, get-rich-quick schemes surfaced throughout America and eventually the world. Children, whose parents had once held with Franklin's views, grew to adulthood believing affluence obtained through deception yielded the best interest. In many cases, fortunately from a moral observation, their attempts were met with dismal failure.

Ben, in the guise of Poor Richard, was speaking from his own experiences and difficulties up to 1730, when he had been a failure through schemes thought to make him "instantly rich." The primary words may have come from such philosophic writers as a Fuller or Bacon, but their reflections were from his own lot.

Not until October of 1730 did he realize his need to follow the plan penned in his journal six years earlier.

When at length he mastered the plan, he resolved to deliver its impressions to readers of his almanac… "That they might achieve some measure of my success, and rise to prominence in the world."

Even Poor Richard wrote of a dire need to succeed in its first issue:

Courteous Reader:

I might in this place attempt to gain thy favor, by declaring that I write almanacks with no other view than that of the publick good; but in this I should not be sincere; and men are now-a-days too wise to be deceiv'd by pretenses, how soever. The plain truth of the matter is, I am excessive poor, and my wife, good woman, is, I tell her, excessive proud; she cannot bear, she says, to sit spinning in her shift of tow [11]; while I do nothing but gaze at the stars;and has threaten'd more than once to burn all my books and rattle-traps (as she calls all my instruments) if I do not make some profitable use of them for the good of my family. The printer has offer'd me some considerable share of the profits, and I have thus begun to comply with my dame's desire.

The buyer of my almanack may consider himself not only as purchasing this useful utensil, but as performing an act of charity, to his poor servant, R. Saunders.

Today, knowing of Ben Franklin's essence as Richard Saunder's alter ego, we can sit back to read this in quiet amusement. But imagine, if you will, the effect it had on the colonials who believed the poor hen-pecked astrologer a real person suffering somewhere within their core. Is it any wonder, then, the first edition should sell out within its initial month, with two extra editions printed to meet the demand? Colonists all over America wanted Poor Richard to succeed if, perchance, it helped them to succeed as well.

The next year's issue saw Poor Richard take an occasion to rejoice in his winning new venture:

Courteous Reader:

Your kind and charitable assistance last year, in purchasing so large an impression of my almanacks, has made my circumstances much more easy in the world, and requires my grateful acknowledgment. My wife has been enabled to get a pot of her own, and is no longer oblig'd to borrow one from a neighbor; not that we ever had something of our own to put in it. She has also got a pair of shoes, two new shifts, and a new petticoat; and for my part, I have purchas'd a second-hand coat, so good that I am not asham'd to go to town, or be seen there. These things have render'd her temper so pacifick than it us'd to be, that I may say I have slept more, and more quietly, within the last year than in the three foregoing years put together. Accept my hearty thanks, therefore, and my sincere wishes for your health and prosperity. R. Saunders.

To this, he added a postscript:

I must not omit here to thank the publick for their generous and kind encouragement they have hereto given me. But if the generous purchaser of my labours could see how often his Fi'pence helps to light up the com-

fortable fire, line the pots, fill the cup, and make glad the heart of a poor man and his good old woman, he would not think his money ill laid out, tho' the almanack of his friend and servant, R. SAUNDERS were one-half blank pages.

The "publick" could hardly wait for the next issue; still another year away.

As the years passed and Poor Richard prospered, so too did his readers. Not only were they shown how to earn extra money, they were given information on making wine from wild grapes and what timber to use for better fencing. They were advised as to weather changes for an abundant crop season; and introduced to a new-style calendar [12].

When *Poor Richard's Almanack* first appeared, it was the eighth almanac in Philadelphia. But by its closing year of 1758 it had surpassed all the almanacs sold throughout the world, with total sales of over a quarter of a million copies.

Even France had taken Poor Richard to heart, renaming him *"Bonhomme Richard."*

The French merchant class, tired of aristocratic heavy-handedness toward individual pursuits, ingested every issue of the translated American almanac.

Meetings were held.

Both merchants and their citizen patrons came together to hear passages brought to life through an assemblage of excited voices. Signs were fashioned highlighting the virtues of *Bonhomme Richard*. "Free enterprise is the way to wealth," a cry went out. "Down with the aristocratic weight of taxes." The people of France had a new hero who would eventually lead them, if in spirit only, to their own revolution.

It is a sad fact that life is not a placid road, even for one as propelled as Ben Franklin. Its dips, valleys and curves can retard the most inalterable course.

In 1736, smallpox struck Philadelphia, and Ben tearfully watched his little 4-year-old Francis Folger succumb to the dreaded disease in November. "Franky, I believe," he confided to a friend fifty years later, "would have been the best of my children."

This is even sadder when we learn that by the time of his son's death he had become a staunch advocate for smallpox inoculations. For fifteen years, since his brother James had fought so fiercely against it in the *Courant*, Ben had wrestled with it in his conscience; and had, by observation, become firmly convinced of its value.

Although English physician Edward Jenner, FRS would not develop a cowpox vaccine for smallpox until 1796, the colonies had been aware of immunization since 1721, when Cotton Mather introduced it to Boston. Boston, however, feared Mather as much as they did the disease. "People," they reasoned, "would die from the disease at any rate."

Ben was too young at the time to effectively argue for or against this conjecture, yet still could not erase the thought that such a preventive measure was possible, gathering over the years data justifying its use. "Dangerous as it would seem to some," he wrote in a paper. "Inoculation is still many times safer than getting the disease."

Just weeks prior to Franky's contracting the smallpox, Ben had praised its treatment in an article for a forthcoming issue of *Poor Richard's Almanack.*

A few weeks into November, he determined to have the child immunized "as soon as my son recover'd from his present illness."

But it was too late. The little one's apparently mild ailment was, in reality, the smallpox.

Debbie, Ben and 6-year-old Willie — the three having been recently immunized — stood at the foot of the tiny bed. Debbie wept openly; Ben, whose deportment had never allowed for tears, felt the strangely warm liquid move gently down his cheeks; Willie stared emotionless, as the doctor covered the body of Francis Folger Franklin.

Subsequent rumors to Franky's having died from the effects of inoculation and not the disease were bitterly arrested in the pages of the *Pennsylvania Gazette.*

In 1759, Ben agreed to write a preface for Dr. William Heberdon's book *Some Accounts of the Success of Inoculation for Small-pox*, to which he systematically presented statistics collected before and since his son's death, concluding that "of the 1,601 inoculated thus far, only six have died." Some years later, Jan Ingenhousz and Gerhard Von Sweitzen, physicians to Empress Maria Theresa [13] and Emperor Joseph II of Austria, consulted with him prior to attempting immunization of the royal family.

By January of 1737, Ben had thrown himself back into business in order to mend a nearly broken heart.

In response to Philadelphia's German populace, he produced the first German language hymnbook in America and founded America's first German newspaper, the *Philadelphia Zeitung.*

In February he published several political pamphlets, imported the finer books from London for sale in his shop; and began franchising his printing business.

Having heard of South Carolina's need for a printer, he sent journeyman Thomas Whitemarsh to Charleston to set a shop in motion, wherein he, Franklin, would pay one-third the expenses and receive one-third the profits. When this experiment proved a success, he expanded to New York and Connecticut.

Interestingly, when Whitemarsh died shortly after commencing the business, his widow took over and ran it until she had amassed enough to purchase the entire Charleston operation and appropriate all of South Carolina's printing.

This so impressed Ben; **B. Franklin** offered to set other women up in business but without much success. The timing, he was to find for that century, was not right.

Perhaps he was thinking of Debbie's proficiency in their own enterprises when he enthusiastically endorsed the "entrepreneurial rights of women." In his seventies, he undoubtedly had her in mind when he wrote "...as long as I was fortunate enough to have a wife, I had adopt'd the habit of letting myself be guid'd by her opinions on difficult matters; for women, I believe, have a certain feeling, which is more reliable than our reasoning."

In 1767, Jane Mecom decided to launch a millinery venture with daughters Jane and Polly.

Ben vigorously approved his sister's project and contacted an old friend in London, who selected the finest ribbons, bonnets and caps for delivery to the new shop. He financed the initial stock with this prediction: "Industry and frugality will eventually make the girls grow rich."

Jane was the most hapless of all the children born to Josiah and Abiah Franklin. Like Ben, who was the youngest son, she was the youngest daughter. Unlike Ben, she was unable to prosper as she grew to maturity.

At the age of 15, she married a nearly illiterate saddler named Edward Mecom and would bear him twelve children; of these she buried eight, along with her husband.

Tragedy and despair would plague Jane throughout the years. Her two surviving sons, Peter and Benny, were successively placed on a farm for the "mentally incompetent."

Her brother foot the bill.

If hardened by life in the world of business, Ben had always been softened by his love for Jane. She was his "particular favorite." Whenever she needed him, he was there; whenever she needed financial or emotional support, she received it without question. He was the oak upon which she leaned.

Still, with this we must say of Jane Mecom. Through all adversities, she tried never to quit. Her will to succeed almost matched that of her famous brother. She was a vivaciously strong woman, doggedly fighting to hold her own in a world seemingly standing against her.

Nevertheless, interfering with her penchant to overcome was a despondent anticipation of further calamities. When this occurred she would turn to her older brother for solace, his well thought out reasoning raising her spirits to again do battle. Once, he wrote this to her: "It may not be amiss to allow ourselves beforehand the enjoyment of some expect'd pleasures, but it is not so well to afflict ourselves with apprehensions of misfortunes that may never arise."

Thus heartened, she would attempt anew to erase the growing stigma that the Mecoms were "Benjamin Franklin's poor Boston relations." Yet, her ill-fated life continued and the stigma kept growing. Whatever she tied, failed. Whatever new venture she went into, folded not long after opening.

Ben offered her money, encouragement, employment for her sons, even a place to live rent free following each disaster. Perhaps he was the cause of her family's debasement, though he simply could not help it. He loved her too much to watch her die of a "broken spirit." Once, after not hearing from her for a time, he worriedly wrote to a mutual advocate in Boston: "How is my poor old sister gone through the winter? For I am afraid she is too cautious of acquainting me with all her difficulties, though I am always willing to relieve her when I am acquaint'd with them." In a letter to her, he wrote: "Buy whatever you need and charge it to me."

So when Jane envisioned a millinery business leading to "greater things," Ben stood by her once again. He cheerfully told the three women "You should not think of this [the business] as a small start, for I had no more to begin the world with."

Business went well from the beginning, thanks to the many women friends Ben sent to the shop. Jane and Jenny bustled to-and-fro, fussing with the bows and ribbons for the ladies' bonnets, while Polly attended the cashbox.

Yet, again tragedy struck. Polly died of tuberculosis in September of 1767. Sweet cherished Polly, who had always "done so much more than she was able." Jane reeled from this blow as never before. Her cry of anguish reached from Boston to Philadelphia, where Debbie feared her sister-in-law's "duble share of sperritts [sic]" would not be enough to sustain her latest loss. Ben immediately wrote Jane, and received this reply of September 19th: "Sorrows roll upon me like the waves of the sea. I am hardly allowed time to fetch my breath. I am broken with breach upon breach, and have now, in the first flow of my grief, been almost ready to say, "What have I more?" But God forbid that I indulge that thought, though I have lost another child. God is sovereign, and I submit."

Relieved his sister was not thinking of taking her life, Ben advised she continue the business "for the sake of Jenny."

Though still tortured with a mother's anguish, Jane saw the logic in her brother's suggestion and kept the shop open.

Yet even in this, her last refuge, there would be no recovery.

The British Government now heavily enforced the Townshend Acts, imposing duties on glass, lead, paint, tea and paper. On October 28, 1767, Boston held a town meeting, in which they angrily resolved to refuse all importations as protests against the bills. Since Jane's supplies came from England, she lamented: "It proves a litle [sic] unlucky for me that our people have taken it into their heads to be so excessive frugal at this time."

Objecting to the resolutions, deploring the impact this would have on "my humble industry," she dispatched a note to her brother for support: "...I should like to have those that do buy, and can afford it, should buy what litle [sic] I have to sell..."

Torn between love for his sister and pride in his countrymen's position on the unlawful taxation issue, Ben answered the note as gently as he could: "It is a little unlucky that the business you are fallen into happens, at present, to be in disgrace of your town meeting; perhaps you should think of some other [business] if the resolutions continue, and are regard'd by the ladies."

That was all she needed to hear. Her beloved brother had turned from her and dealt the final blow.

She was tired. Tired of fighting, and tired of losing.

Even Ben's offer to help her find another enterprise did no good. The damage had already been done. After settling her accounts, she locked the shop's door for the last time and left Boston.

Ben and Jane eventually reunited. Nevertheless, Jane could never quite forgive him his one "disloyalty" toward her; and Ben had never forgiven himself. He did everything to make her "last days" as comfortable as he possibly could since, "given her now tender constitution," he was sure he would outlive his sorely prostrated younger sister.

Surprisingly, she was to survive him by four years, never knowing her brother's "disloyalty" was a soul-rending clash between political views and personal feelings.

By 1738, Ben was in public office as clerk for the Pennsylvania General Assembly and musing over an uncommon business expansion.

Recognizing a new population boom in Philadelphia, he bought whatever houses had "To Let" signs hanging in windows and rented them out at rates lower than former owners were asking. This arrangement added even greater to his already substantial income. But more importantly, it helped to relieve the rising homeless crises suffered by the city's overcrowding.

The year 1739 passed rather uneventfully for Ben. His enterprises were thriving; he was still clerk of the Assembly; and Willie kept his fatherly juices flowing. Yet, he was restless; as if all were a waste of his time, his fertile mind showing signs of sterility. That year, he was often seen walking the streets late at night "...looking as if he knew not where he was going, nor from whence he came."

By 1740, he had regained his direction. That year the Franklin stove was invented [14].

On one cold, wintry afternoon, Ben was on duty as a librarian for the Philadelphia Library. The same free circulating library he had founded so cunningly in 1731. Over the years it had grown steadily, with rows upon rows of high quality books for subscribers to choose from. The books were ordered through Peter Collinson, a Quaker merchant living in London. Collinson would send over a well-selected assortment, occasionally adding a few gift volumes for his friend, Ben Franklin.

Ben was reading one of the gifts, Richard Bentley's *The Boyle Lectures*, as closing time approached. Debbie should still be working on the shop's inventory and would not be finished for another three hours. This would give him enough time to hurry home and complete the book in front of the light and warmth of his fireplace without interruption. Willie was spending the night with a neighboring companion.

As Ben sat in front of the fireplace reflectively reading the treatise he had never had time to finish as a boy, he felt a cold draft on his back. His face was baking, while his spine suffered an oppressive chill. Placing the book down, he stood and walked from the fireplace. Freezing!

This proved a hypothesis he had discussed with his Junto members two Fridays ago, yet had no time to study. Now he did.

When Debbie walked up the stairs from the shop and into the room, the fireplace was dark and Ben had his head up the chimney. She smiled to herself, turned, and went to bed. "Pappy's up to something again," she must have thought.

"Our familiar fireplace," he observed in notes preserved over time, "might have the comfort of two warm seats, one on each corner; but they are sometimes too hot to abide in, and the cold air so nips the back and heels of those that sit before the fire that they have no comfort..." In keeping with his frugal nature, he also observed: "A moderate quantity of wood on the fire, in so large a hearth seems but a little; and in so strong and cold a draft, warms but little; so that people are continually laying on more. In short, it is next to impossible to warm a room with such a fireplace."

The solution: Ben combined the German stove, which had the benefit of warming an entire room when placed in the center, with the open fireplace.

The drawback to the German stove was that it showed no fire, nor did it bring in fresh air. Ben wished not to lose the benefit of fire, "which in itself is a pleasant thing," and fresh air would be necessary "to keep us from suffocating." He solved both problems by placing his stove in the middle of the fireplace, thus retaining "the sight of fire." The rising heat was made to descend and circulate before finding vent up the chimney, allowing for fresh air currents to warm as they entered the room.

His friend Robert Grace, who now managed the Warwick Furnace Company, manufactured the stove to Ben's specifications.

The next step was a 1744 advertisement, in which Ben endorsed it in a little booklet entitled: *An Account of the newly-invented Pennsylvania Fireplaces*.

Swayed by the colonies' enthusiasm for the new stove, Pennsylvania's Lieutenant Governor George Thomas proposed Ben apply for an exclusive patent, which he declined on the grounds that: "As we enjoy great advantage from the inventions of others, we should be glad to serve others by any inventions of ours; and this we should do freely and generously."

But not everyone was inclined to such scruples.

In London, an ironmonger [15] literally stole the plans for Benjamin Franklin's stove, applied for and received a patent, and made a small fortune. "This," recorded Ben years later, "is not the only instance of patents taken out for my inventions by others, tho' not always with the same success, which I never contested, as having no desire of profiting by patents myself, and hating disputes."

1741 and 1742 passed into 1743.

Debbie gave birth to a daughter she would name Sarah. And Ben founded the American Philosophical Society, dedicated to the advancement of science and the humanities.

In 1744, William made his first bid for freedom in an attempt to head for the high seas, but was collared by his father on the deck of a privateer before the ship sailed off.

Amused, rather than angered, Ben drolly thought back to his own youth and ruffled the boy's windblown hair. How quickly the younger becomes the older generation.

All the way home, William complained of Deborah. Her barbed tongue and short-tempered actions frightened him at times. Was she really that angry with him? What had he done to deserve her abusive behavior? If he had a chance, he would run away again.

Ben placed his arm gently on his son's shoulder, laughed, and told him not to worry. "Debbie," he said, "is just that way. She means nothing by it."

This was the façade he wished his son and the world to see.

In reality he knew his wife, if accepting William, resented his illegitimacy. Too, she could not abide his paying more attention to William than his own 1-year-old daughter.

But William was a boy, he reasoned. A boy who was interested in his father's experiments. Should not boys be close to their fathers, and girls their mothers? Besides, though pompous at times, Willie was a good lad. He would have to discuss this with Debbie. Such animosity, for whatever reason, will drive their son further away.

In November of 1745, three men labored over an experiment at Holland's University of Leiden [Leyden]. They were Professor Musschenbroek, Professor Allemand, and a friend named Andreas Cuneus. For weeks they had endeavored to expand on tests conducted by the professors DuFay, Hawksbee, Von Guericks and Gilbert to induce electrical current with sparks and flashes.

In theory, flashes were of the same nature as lightning, but this supposition, however plausible, had never been ascertained. The three Dutchmen had succeeded in producing electricity by friction, yet still failed in finding a solution for retaining it. The power leaked away as swiftly as it gathered.

Professor Musschenbroek decided a wide-mouth container in the form of a glass bottle half filled with water was necessary as a solution to this dilemma. In effect, he had mistakenly concluded over the past few days, this device would allow the water to serve as the conductor, while the glass would function as a non-conductor.

One end of a wire, leading from the bottle to the laboratory's friction machine, was dipped into the water with no reaction. Then Mr. Cuneus accidentally touched one hand to the machine while resting the other on the bottle's glass surface, resulting in "a shock heard round the world." He jerked unconscious to the floor with the first recorded electric shock created by a man-made contrivance.

The two professors later purposely repeated the mishap and were both knocked cold. An electrical charge had been contained within a seemingly innocent glass bottle, and the world of the 18th century would never be the same.

The Leyden jar, as French physicist Jean-Antoine Nollet later named it, became the sensation of the scientific community. News of its conquest over the elusive element of electricity carried throughout the European continent.

In the pseudo-scientific world quacks and itinerant medicine shows declared electricity the cure for all ailments, the restorer of lost hair and "the dispeller of double chins."

Even charlatans beheld the Leyden jar as better than alchemy. According to their claims, it converted an invisible force into gold coins.

In 1746, Ben visited his mother in Boston. His father had died the previous year and this was his first chance to pay respects.

Still, even on this sad occasion, his mind could not be spoiled from business. He scouted several shops to learn of new developments in the printing trade.

While visiting one of the shops, he witnessed an amazing little performance by Dr. Archibald Spencer, a Scottish physician and wandering showman, whom he had met on a trip to Boston three years earlier. Dr. Spencer was demonstrating the use of "modern electricity" as dramatized with an electric tube [16]. This tube, when rubbed with buck-skin, infused objects with electricity.

Ben was as excited as the day he first opened his print shop with Hugh Meredith. From that moderate exhibition he was lost for a time to all other pursuits, save for that of the "electrician."

In 1747, back home in Philadelphia, Ben received his own electric tube from London's Peter Collinson and began "playing with it" from dawn until long after dusk. "I never was before engag'd in any study," he wrote, "that so totally engross'd my attention and my time as this has largely done for, what with making experiments when I can be alone, and repeating them to friends and acquaintances, who, from the novelty of the thing, come continually in crowds to see them, I have, during some months past, had little leisure for anything else."

But, before long, Ben's mind and time would train themselves in a different direction. Talk of an encompassing war had reached Pennsylvania. His electrical tests would need placing aside for some future date.

The colonies had been drawn into England's latest war with France when a New England British force captured the French Fortress Louisbourg on Cape Breton Island in June of 1745. The French, in retaliation, first attacked the American Continent itself by destroying the village of Saratoga, New York; directing their Indian allies to slay the inhabitants indiscriminately.

Ben recommended Philadelphia establish a line of resistance, believing French troops would push down from Canada and lay further assaults on the open colonies of Pennsylvania.

When met with diminished enthusiasm by the Quaker-ruled Assembly, who had no wish to participate in "King George's War," he issued a 22-page pamphlet titled *Plain Truth*, in which he hoped to arouse the people themselves.

In a conservative, yet somewhat exasperated manner, he wrote:

> **What must be your condition if suddenly surpris'd, without previous alarm, perhaps in the night! ...Your best fortunes will be to fall under the power of commanders of the King's ships, able to control the mariners, and so into the hands of *Licentious Privateers* who, can, without the utmost horror, conceive the miseries of the latter, when your persons, fortunes, wives, and daughters shall be subject to the unbridled rage, rapine, and the lust of the vilest and most abandoned of mankind? A dred scene! ...We, the middling people, cannot fly with our families; and if we could how shall we subsist? No, we must bear the brunt...**

The full text of *Plain Truth* agitated the public into calling a town meeting, which ultimately allowed for the formation of Pennsylvania's first militia. Within weeks nearly ten thousand volunteers joined. Money was raised through a lottery for the purchase of guns from Boston, and for the construction of an efficient battery. Next came the need for more cannon. The few rusted pieces of artillery they had acquired from a Boston foundry were not enough so a committee of three, which included our friend Ben Franklin, was chosen to borrow some from New York's provincial governor and England's rear Admiral, George Clinton.

Governor Clinton at first refused, protesting New York's lack of any cannon to spare. But Ben, in his way, had his way and, following a night of tippling a fine Madeira wine, Clinton would have given away the entire executive mansion.

Ben tells it best in his own words:

"He [Clinton] at first refus'd us peremptorily; but at dinner with his council, where there was great drinking of a Madeira wine as the custom of that place then was, he soften'd by degrees, and said he would lend us six. After a few more bumpers he advanc'd to ten; and at length he very good-natur'dly conced'd eighteen. They were fine cannon, 18-pounders, with their carriages, which we soon transport'd and mount'd on our battery, where the Associators [militia] kept a nightly guard while the war last'd, and among the remainder I regularly took my turn of duty as a common soldier."

Although offered the rank of colonel in his Pennsylvania regiment, Ben preferred to fight as a foot soldier until peace was signed at Aix-la-Chapelle in 1748.

So Ben's first taste of war came to an end in 1748. So, too, did his entrepreneurial career.

At the age of 42, with a business worth £2,000 per year, he was ready to retire and relax to a semi-active private life.

David Hall, his four-year foreman and husband to Debbie's cousin, was brought in as an operative partner and executive director for his printing shop in Philadelphia.

This partnership would continue harmoniously for eighteen years. And, within that duration, would yield Ben an average retirement income of £400.67 per annum.

Add to this his paid political offices, his franchise connections in New York and Connecticut and his real estate holdings; he was indeed a wealthy man for the times. His proceeds even surpassed that of the royal governor of Pennsylvania, whose annual resource accorded him £1000.

In September of 1748, he wrote to a friend: "I am in a fair way of having no other tasks than such as I shall like to give myself, and of enjoying what I look upon as a great happiness; leisure to read, study, and make experiments, and converse at large with such ingenious and worthy men as are pleas'd to honour me with their friendship or acquaintance, or such points as may produce something for the common benefit of mankind, uninterrupt'd by the little cares and fatigues of business."

Nineteen months later, in April of 1750, he wrote to his mother: "At present I pass my time agreeably enough. I enjoy, thro' mercy, a tolerable share of health. I read a great deal, ride a little, do a little business for myself, and now and then for others, retire when I can, go into company when I please; so the years roll 'round, and the last will come, when I would rather have it said, 'He liv'd usefully, than 'he dy'd rich'.""

In less than two years of retirement, Ben Franklin was battling an uneasy feeling of sterility. A perception he knew would kill him long before his time; and that death, he also knew, would stem from a wasted life.

One evening, two weeks after the letter to his mother, Debbie was cleaning Ben's study and happened upon a remark he had recently scribbled on a scrap of paper:

If you would not be forgott'n as soon as you are dead, and rott'n, either write things worth the reading, or do things worth the writing.

Recognizing this as advice given by Poor Richard to his readers back in 1738, she clutched the note heavily and dabbed away tears with her apron.

The next day, she placed the crinkled paper in the palm of Ben's hand.

"Pappy," she said softly. "You will do things worth the writing."

"My dear Debbie."

Ben placed his arms around her and kissed her gently on each cheek.

Drawing away as if angry with him again, she turned to leave the room.

"You have conquered the world of business, Benjamin Franklin," she bellowed over her shoulder. "Now you have the rest of the world to conquer. Do not mope round here any longer. I will not have it!"

And conquer the rest of the world he did — for us all!

But that's for another story.

Epilogue

When Benjamin Franklin passed into history at the age of 84, he left an estimated estate worth $150,000; owned several houses in Philadelphia and Boston, lands in Georgia, Ohio and Nova Scotia; and held bonds, bank shares and securities amounting to $25,000.

Of his descendants, none are alive who bear the name Franklin.

William Franklin died leaving one son, William Temple.

"Temple" Franklin fathered a son, Theophile, by a mistress named Blanchette Caillot in 1785. The boy died in 1787. Temple then took his father's second wife's sister, Ellen Johnson D'evelin, and produced an illegitimate daughter named Ellen in 1798. Nineteen days prior to his May 25, 1823 death, he married Hannah Collyer in Paris, France. No child was born to this union.

Ellen Franklin married a Capel Hanbury on June 8, 1818, and had a daughter Marie. Ellen passed away on February 21, 1875 in Nice, France, without bearing another child. Marie Hanbury died unmarried and childless, ending the line for William and Temple Franklin.

Sarah Franklin Bache, Ben's daughter, bore numerous offspring, but none of her lineage can follow a direct trail back to the self-made man of the ages.

Ben Franklin started with little but his native talent. He faltered, yet persevered until achieving the material prosperity he knew could be his, extending to a distinguished career as a scientist, statesman and diplomat.

He departed this world with no regrets, giving us this observation of his life:

"Whether I have been doing good or mischief is for time to discover. I only know that I intend'd well and I hope that all will end well."

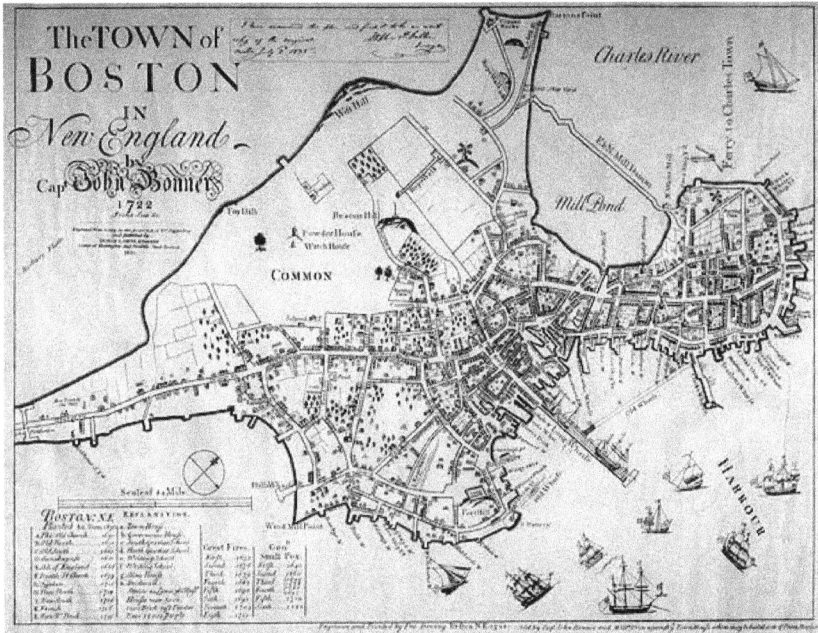

Captain John Bonner's Map of Boston, 1722.
Courtesy:
Rotch Library Map Collection
Massachusetts Institute of Technology
77 Massachusetts Avenue
Cambridge, MA 02139

Ben's birthplace on 17 Milk Street, situated between Marlborough [now Washington] and Hawley Streets, Boston.

This house stood across from Cedar Meeting House [now Old South Meeting House], where the infant was baptized on the day of his birth, Sunday, January 6th [old style calendar, January 17th, new style].

Abiah Franklin attended services that morning, went home to give birth about noon, and returned that afternoon for the baptism.

Artwork courtesy:
Massachusetts Institute of Technology
77 Massachusetts Avenue
Cambridge, MA 02139

Ben at work [right] as apprentice to his brother James.
Artwork courtesy:
U.S. National Archives and
Records Administration
8601 Adelphi Road
College Park, MD 20740

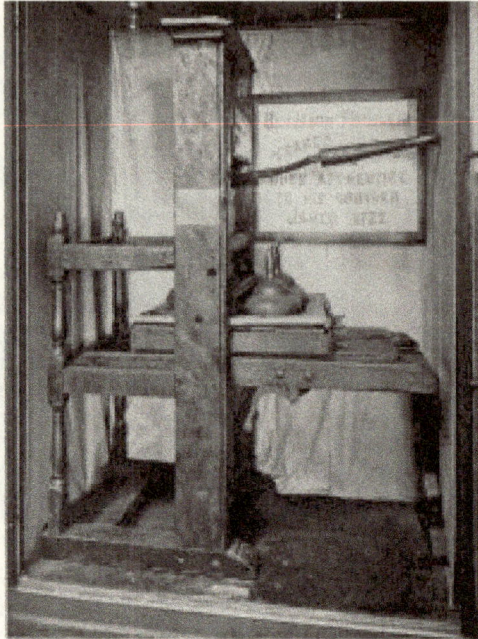

The plaque in this photo reads: "Benjamin Franklin worked on this printing press when apprenticed to his brother James in 1722."

Photo courtesy:
U.S. National Archives and
Records Administration
8601 Adelphi Road
College Park, MD 20740

When Ben Franklin entered Philadelphia on Sunday, October 6, 1723, he was a tattered, hungry, 17-year-old boy with one Dutch dollar to his name, munching on a stale roll. Twenty-five years later he had garnered enough money for a comfortable retirement. [Note: Deborah Read is seen on the right, gleefully observing his entrance into the city.]

Artwork courtesy:
U.S. National Archives and
Records Administration
8601 Adelphi Road
College Park, MD 20740

Ben's shop on High Street [now Market Street].

    Within this edifice grew the *Pennsylvania Gazette* and *Poor Richard's Almanack*. It also held a stationery, book and general store, where shoppers could purchase anything from writing materials to books, to ointments and salves compounded by Debbie's mother, to bars of soap manufactured in Boston by Ben's brother John.

    The Franklins made their home above the shop until Ben's formal retirement in 1748.

Ben makes notes for *Poor Richard's*, ca 1740.
Artwork courtesy:
U.S. National Archives and
Records Administration
8601 Adelphi Road
College Park, MD 20740

Deborah Read Rogers Franklin, ca 1766
(1708 – 1774)
She was to Ben a "…good and faithful helpmate. We throve together and have mutually endeavor'd to make each other happy."

Ben Franklin's famous kite experiment of 1752.
Artwork courtesy:
U.S. National Archives and
Records Administration
8601 Adelphi Road
College Park, MD 20740

William Franklin, ca 1793
(1731 – 1813)
He chose to remain loyal to Britain during the Revolutionary Turmoil.

Portrait courtesy:
American Philosophical Society
104 South Fifth Street
Philadelphia, PA 19106

Ben Franklin at the Court of Versailles, France, ca 1777.
Artwork courtesy:
U.S. National Archives and
Records Administration
8601 Adelphi Road
College Park, MD 20740

Benjamin Franklin, ca 1780
(1706 – 1790)
Portrait courtesy:
American Philosophical Society
104 South Fifth Street
Philadelphia, PA 19106

Sarah Franklin Bache
(1743 – 1808)
Sarah Bache (called Sally) attended her father during his last illness.

A perennial peacemaker, she had a hand in partially reconciling Ben and William six years before their father's death.

The Philadelphia Library moved into this newly constructed building in 1790, the year of Ben's death.   The niche above the door contains a statue of its founder.

Ben rests at Christ Church Burial Ground, Philadelphia. Beside him lies his wife, Debbie. Beside them both lay 4-year-old Francis Folger Franklin, Sarah Franklin Bache and her husband, Richard Bache.

"I wake up every morning at nine and grab for the morning paper. Then I look at the obituary page. If my name is not on it, I get up."

Benjamin Franklin
(1706 – 1790)

Ben Franklin's Times
~A Chronology~

1706

Ben is born in Boston, Massachusetts, January 6th [old style], January 17th [new style calendar]. Baptized at Cedar Meeting House [now Old South Meeting House].

1714

George I rules England [1714-27].

1716

Ben works for his father, Josiah, in candle making [tallow candler] and soap boiling shop [1716-18].

1717

Ben invents swimming fins [placed on hands instead of feet].

1718

Ben is apprenticed to his brother James.

1721

First issue of *The New-England Courant* is published on Monday, August 7th. [Note: This date had been erroneously maintained as Monday, August 17th in many publications for over two hundred years. However, latest research has proved this a misprint, since August 17, 1721 did not fall on Monday in the old style.]

1722

"Silence Dogood" letters are published in *The New-England Courant* [April-October].

1723

Ben leaves Boston. Arrives in Philadelphia.

1724

Ben sails for England on the *London Hope*.   Becomes printer in London [1724-26].

1725

Ben writes and publishes *A Dissertation on Liberty and Necessity, Pleasure and Pain.*

1726

Ben returns to Philadelphia. Begins journal aboard ship, and adds plan for "future conduct in life."

1727

Ben becomes mercantile clerk.   Forms the Junto [forerunner of the American Philosophical Society].   George II becomes king of England [1727-60].

1728

Ben become part owner of a printing business with Hugh Meredith [**FRANKLIN and MEREDITH**].

1729

Ben begins publishing the *Pennsylvania Gazette* [Thursday, September 25th — Thursday, October 2nd]. Takes sole ownership of the printing business [**B. FRANKLIN**].

1730

Takes Deborah Read Rogers as his wife [September 1st].

1731

Ben's illegitimate son, William, is born. Founds the Library of Philadelphia [first circulating library in American colonies, July 1st].

1732

George Washington is born on February 11th [old style calendar], February 22nd, [new style]. Advertisement for the first edition of *Poor Richard's Almanack* [for the year 1733] appears in the *Pennsylvania Gazette* on October 19th [old style]. Ben's son, Francis Folger, is born on October 20th [old style].

1736

Ben forms first organized fire department [Union Fire Company]. Francis Folger Franklin dies of smallpox.

1737

Ben is appointed clerk for Pennsylvania General Assembly

1740

Ben invents the Franklin stove [Pennsylvania Fireplace]. Designated official printer for New Jersey.

1743

Ben first draws up *Proposals Relating to the Education of Youth in Pennsylvania*, but King George's War forestalled it until 1749, when a published version prompts established classes for the Academy and College of Philadelphia on August 13th 1751. Daughter, Sarah, is born on September 11th [old style]. Founds the American Philosophical Society.

1744

Ben advertises the Franklin stove through a booklet entitled: *An Account of the newly-invented Pennsylvania Fireplaces*.

1747

Ben begins electrical experiments. Writes and publishes the pamphlet *Plain Truth*, which aids in the formation of Pennsylvania's first militia.

1748

Ben retires from active business life.

1749
Ben is appointed president of the Academy and College of Philadelphia on November 13th,and prepares for its opening on August 13, 1751. Becomes Justice of the Peace for Philadelphia.

1751
Ben writes *Experiments and Observations on Electricity, Made at Philadelphia in America*. Helps to establish classes for the Academy and College of Philadelphia [predecessor to the University of Pennsylvania] on August 13th. Founds [with Dr. Thomas Bond] the Pennsylvania Hospital. Elected to the Pennsylvania Assembly. Writes and publishes *Observations Concerning the Increase of Mankind*.

1752
Ben completes dangerous electrical experiment with kite

during thunderstorm [June 15th]. Places first lightning rod used in America on the roof of his home. Creates the first fire insurance company in America. Invents the medical catheter to help his extremely ill brother John.

1753

Ben writes description of the lightning rod. Receives honorary Master of Arts degrees from Harvard and Yale universities. Awarded Copley Medal of the Royal Society [London] for his work in electricity. Appointed North America's Deputy Postmaster General [with William Hunter of Virginia]. French sent to occupy the Ohio Valley.

1754

Ben creates the first political cartoon in North America [JOIN or DIE], which appeared in the *Pennsylvania Gazette* [May 9th]. Presents "Plan of Union" at Albany Congress. Aids British General Edward Braddock in defending Pennsylvania against Indian attacks. First action of French and Indian War [1754-63]. Americans defeated at Fort Necessity.

1755

In the middle of a dispute between the Penns and Quakers [historically recognized as Braddock's Campaign], General Edward Braddock is killed in battle at Monongahela

[July 15th]. An earthquake shakes Boston [November 18th].

1756

Ben leads Philadelphia volunteers to western Pennsylvania. Elected Fellow of the Royal Society. Named Postmaster General of North America. Seven Years War in Europe begins [1756-63].

1757

Ben goes to London, as agent for the Pennsylvania Assembly, to plead against the Proprietors [Penns]. Writes *The Way to Wealth*.

1759

Ben visits northern England and Scotland. Receives honorary Doctor of Laws degree from the University of St. Andrews [Scotland]. British General James Wolfe defeats the French General Louis-Joseph de Montcalm at the Plains of Abraham, near Quebec City, New France [September 13th], with both generals mortally wounded during the battle.

1760

Ben writes *Interests of Great Britain Considered*. Receives Privy Council approval for taxation of proprietary estates in Pennsylvania. George III crowned king of England

[1760 – 1820].

1761

Ben invents the glass armonica [as opposed to the "harmonica," invented in the 19th century], one of the most celebrated musical instruments in the 18th century.

1762

Ben receives honorary Doctor of Civil Laws degree from Oxford University [Oxford, England]. Returns to Philadelphia. William Franklin is appointed royal governor of New Jersey through help from his father.

1763

Ben tours the northern colonies to inspect post offices. Pontiac's Uprising [Pontiac's Rebellion, 1763-66]. The Paxton Incident [in opposition to Pontiac's Rebellion].

1764

Ben pushes the Militia Bill. Drafts petition for changes in the government. Defeated for re-election to the Assembly. Returns to England as agent for Pennsylvania. Charts the Gulf Stream [mapped]. England enforces the Stamp Act [reinvigoration of the Molasses Act of 1733]. Committees of Correspondence formed to protest taxation without representation.

1766

Ben testifies before House of Commons to repeal England's Stamp Act. Stamp Act repealed [March 18th].

1767

Ben visits France. England imposes the Townshend Acts on July 2nd, enveloping duties on glass, lead, paint, tea and paper [all imported in large quantities by America].

1768

Ben writes the article *Causes of American Discontent Before 1768*, published in the *London Chronicle*. Appointed agent for Georgia.

1769

Ben is elected president of the American Philosophical Society [re-elected annually for life]. Named agent for New Jersey.

1770

Ben becomes agent for Massachusetts. Conducts newspaper campaign against the Townshend Acts. Boston Massacre [March 5th]. Townshend Acts repealed [except on tea] in April.

1771

Ben begins writing his autobiography in the form of a long letter to his son William at the country home of Jonathan Shipley, bishop of St.Asaph, England. Tours Ireland.

1773

England enforces the Tea Act. Boston Tea Party [December 16th].

1774

Ben is called to a hearing before the Privy Council. Dismissed as Postmaster General. England passes the Coercive Acts. [Note: As punishment for the Boston Tea Party, these acts closed Boston's ports, the capital was moved to Salem, town meetings were curbed and political freedom in Massachusetts fettered.] The First Continental Congress convenes in secret [September 5th—October 26th] to protest the Intolerable Acts [Coercive Acts]. Galloway's "Plan of Union" is defeated. Louis XVI becomes king of France [1774-92]. Deborah Franklin dies [December 19th].

1775

Ben returns to Philadelphia. Invents an odometer to help measure mileage of routes used for delivering mail. Elected to First Continental Congress. Offers "Articles of Confederation of United Colonies." Paul Revere, with William Dawes and Samuel Prescott, rides to warn the colonies of a British invasion [April 18th-19th]. Battles of Lexington and Concord [April 19th]. Ticonderoga [Fort Ticonderoga] taken from the British by Ethan Allen's Green Mountain Boys [May 10th]. Battle of Bunker Hill [actually fought on nearby Breed's Hill], where the British defeat American colonial forces [June 17th].

1776

British evacuate Boston [March 17th]. Ben signs the Declaration of Independence. [Note: Although the Declaration of Independence was adopted on July 4th, a decisive transcript was not signed until August 2nd.] Americans forced to retreat from Long Island and New York City [September 15th]. Ben sails for France as commissioner to negotiate alliances. The Battle of Trenton ends in victory for General George Washington [December 26th].

1777

Battles of Saratoga [September 19th & October 7th]. Ben is lionized by Parisian society. Congress accepts "Articles of Confederation of United Colonies."

1778

Ben signs Treaty of Aliance with France. John Adams arrives in Paris. British evacuate Philadelphia [June 18th]. John Paul Jones successfully raids British waters.

1779

Ben is appointed minister to the French court. Spain declares war on England in support of the American colonies [June 16th]. John Paul Jones wins America's first major naval victory, which convinces France to bankroll the colonies further [September 23rd]. John Jay named minister to Madrid, Spain [September 27th].

1780

John Paul Jones returns triumphantly to America aboard the *Ariel* [December 18th].

1781

Ben is appointed to peace commission with John Adams and John Jay; and Thomas Jefferson, who remained in America [June 18th]. Surrender of British General Charles Cornwallis' army at Yorktown, Virginia seals America's independence [articles of capitulation signed October 19th].

1783

A decisive peace treaty is signed with England [Treaty of Paris, September 3rd]. British evacuate New York City [November 25th].

1784

United States Congress Assembled approves the Treaty of Paris, formally ending America's fight for independence [January 14th]. Ben develops glasses known universally as bifocals. Proposes the idea of a Daylight Saving Time in an essay entitled "An Economic Project." Negotiates treaties of commerce with European nations. John Jay is appointed Secretary of Foreign Affairs [1784-90].

1785

John Adams and Thomas Jefferson are appointed ministers to England and France, respectively. Ben returns to Philadelphia. Elected to the presidency of the Pennsylvania Supreme Executive Council.

1786

Ben contrives the "Long Arm" ["The Grabber"], an extension device for taking books down from high shelves. Shays' Rebellion brings on changes to the original Constitution at the Constitutional Convention of 1787.

1787

Ben attends the Constitutional Convention in Philadelphia to deliberate amendments to the original Constitution. [May 25th-September 17th].

1788

Amended Constitution ratified [June 21st]. First Federal elections held from December 15, 1788 – January 10, 1789.

1789

George Washington and John Adams are chosen for the new country's highest offices [January 10th]. Ben is president of the newly incorporated **Pennsylvania Society for the Abolition of Slavery, and the Relief of Free Negroes Unlawfully Held in Bondage** [as his last public service]. The First Federal Congress convenes [March 4th]. Adams is inaugurated vice president on April 21st. Washington takes the oath on April 30th. Final draft to the Constitution is adopted [April 30th]. The French Revolution begins, arguably with the storming of the Bastille, Paris [July 14th].

1790

Alexander Hamilton, as America's first Secretary of the

Treasury, submits *First Report on Public Credit* [January 14th]. Thomas Jefferson takes oath of office as Secretary of State [March 22nd]. Ben Franklin dies in Philadelphia at the age of 84 [April 17th].

Appendix A

To-day's Calendar Introduc'd
(Original preface to *Poor Richard Improved*, 1752)

Kind Reader,

Since the king and parliament have thought fit to alter one year, by taking eleven days out of September 1752, and directing us to begin our account for the future on the first of January, some account of the changes the year has heretofore undergone, and the reasons of them, may a little gratify thy curiosity.

The vicissitude of seasons seems to have given occasion to the first institution of the year. Man, naturally curious to know the cause of that diversity, soon found it was the nearness and distance of the sun; and upon this, gave the name year to the space of time wherein that luminary, performing his whole course, return'd to the same point of his orbit.

And hence, as it was on account of the seasons, that the year was institut'd, their chief regard and attention was, that the same parts of the year should always correspond to the same season; i.e. that the beginning of the year should always be when the sun was in the same point of his orbit; and that they should keep pace, come 'round, and end together.

This, different nations aim'd to attain by different ways; making the year to commence from different points of the zodiac; and even the time of his progress different. So that some of their years were more perfect than others, but none of them quite just; i.e. none of them but whose parts shifted with regard to the parts of the sun's course.

It was the Egyptians, if we may credit Herodotus, that first form'd the year, making it to contain 360 days, which they subdivided into twelve months, of thirty days each.

Mercury Trismegistus added five days more. And on this footing Thales is said to have institut'd the year among the Greeks. Tho' that form of year did not hold throughout all Greece. Add that the Roman, Jewish, Syrian, Arabic, Persian, &c. years, are all different.

Hence, in considering the poor state of astronomy in those ages, it is no wonder different people should disagree in the calculus of the sun's course. We are even assured by Diodorus Siculus, Plutarch, and Pliny, that the Egyptian year itself was at first different from what it became afterw'ds.

According to our account, the Solar Year, or the interval of time in which the sun finishes his course thro' the zodiac, and returns to the same point thereof from which it depart'd is 365 days, 5 hours, 48 minutes, tho' some astronomers make it a few seconds, and some a whole minute less; as Kepler, for instance, who makes it 365 days, 5 hours, 48 minutes, 57 seconds, 39 thirds.   Ricciolus, 365 days, 5 hours, 48 minutes. Tycho Brahe, 365 days, 5 hours, 48 minutes.

The Civil Year is that form of year in which each nation has contriv'd to compute time by; or the Civil is the Tropical Year, consider'd as only consisting of a certain number of whole days; the odd hours and minutes being set aside, to render the computation of time in the common occasion of life more easy.

Hence as the Tropical Year is 365 days, 5 hours, 49 minutes; the Civil Year is 365 days. And hence also, as it is necessary to keep pace with the heavens, it is requir'd that every fourth year consist of 366 days, which would keep the year exactly right, if the odd hours of each year were precesely 6.

The ancient Roman Year, as was first settl'd by Romulus, consist'd of ten months only; viz. I. March, containing 31 days. II. April, 30. III. May, 31. IV. June, 30. V. Quintilis, 31. VI. Sextilis, 30. VII. September, 30. VIII. October, 31. IX. November, 30. X. December, 30; in all 304 days; which came short of the Solar Year, by 61 days.

Hence the beginning of Romulus's year was vague, and unfix'd to any precise season; which inconvenience to remove, that prince order'd so many days to be add'd yearly, as would make the state of the heavens correspond to the first month, without incorporating these additional days; or calling them by the name of any month.

Numa Pompilius correct'd this irregular constitution of the year, and compos'd two new months, January and February, of the days that were to be us'd to be add'd to the former year. Thus, Numa's year consist'd of twelve months; viz. I. January, containing 29 days. II. February, 28. III. March, 31. IV. April, 29. V. May, 31. VI. June, 29. VII. Quintilis, 31. VIII. Sextilis, 29. IX. September, 29, X. October, 31. XI. November, 29. XII. December, 29; in all 355 days, which came short of the common Solar Year by 10 days; so that its beginning was vague and unfix'd.

Numa, however, desiring to have it fix'd up to the Winter Solstice, order'd 22 days to be intercalat'd in February every second year, 22 every fourth, 22 every sixth, and 23 every eight year.

But this rule failing to keep matters even, recourse was had to a new way of intercalating; and instead of 23 days every eighth year, only 15 days were add'd; and the care of the whole committ'd to the Pontilifex Maximus, or high priest; who, neglecting the trust, let things run to the utmost confusion. And thus the Roman Year stood till Julius Caesar made a reformation.

The Julian Year, is a Solar Year, containing commonly 365 days; tho' every fourth year, called Bissextile, contains 366... The names and order of the months of the Julian Year, and the number of days in each, are well-known to us, having been long in use.

The astronomical quantity, therefor, of the Julian Year, is 365 days, 6 hours, which exceeds the true Solar Year by 11 minutes; which excess in 131 years amounts to a whole day... And thus the Roman Year stood, till the reformation made therein by Pope Gregory.

Julius Caesar, in the contrivance of his form of the year, was assist'd by Sosigenes, a famous mathematician, call'd over from Egypt for this purpose; who, to supply the defect of 67 days which had been lost thro' the fault of the high priest, and to fix the beginning of the year to the Winter Solstice, made that year to consist of 15 months, or 455 days, which for that reason is us'd to be call'd Annus Confusionis, the year of Confusion.

This form of the year was us'd by all Christian nations, till the middle of the 16th century; and still continues to be so by several nations;among the rest, by the Swedes, Danes, &c. and by the English till the second of September next, when they are to assume the use of the Gregorian Year.

The Gregorian Year is the Julian Year correct'd by this rule; that whereas on the common footing, every secular or hundredth year, is Bissextile; on the new footing, three of them are common years, and only the fourth Bissextile.

The error of eleven minutes in the Julian Year, little as it was, yet, by being repeat'd over and over, at length became considerable; and from the time when Caesar made his correction, was grown into 13 days, by which the equinoxes were greatly disturb'd. To remedy this irregularity, which was still a-growing, Pope Gregory the XIII, call'd together the chief astronomers of his time, and concert'd that correction; and to restore the equinoxes to their place threw out the ten days that had been got from the Council of Nice, and which had shift'd the fifth of October to the 15th.

In the year 1700,the error of ten days was grown to eleven; upon which the Protestant states of Germany, to prevent further confusions, accept'd the Gregorian correction. And now in 1752, the English follow their example.

Yet is the Gregorian Year far from being perfect, for we have shewn, that, in four centuries, the Julian Year gains 3 days, 1 hour, 20 minutes; but it is only the three days that are kept out in the Gregorian Year; so that here is still an excess of one hour, twenty minutes, in four centuries; which in 72 centuries will amount to a whole day.

As to the commencement of the year, the legal year in England us'd to begin on the day of the annunciation; i.e. on the 25th of March; tho' the historical year began on the day of the circumcision; i.e. the first of January, on which day the Italian and German year also begins; and on which day ours is to begin from this time forward, the first day of January being now by act of Parliament declar'd the first day of the year 1752.

At the yearly meeting of the people call'd Quakers, held in London, since the passing of the act, it was agreed to re-commend to their friends a conformity thereto, by omitting the eleven days of September, and beginning the year there-after on the first day of the month call'd January, which is henceforth to be call'd and written, The First Month, and the rest likewise in their order, so that September will now be the ninth month, December the twelfth.

In wishing withal, according to ancient custom, that this NEW YEAR (which is indeed a new year, such an one as we nev'r saw before, and shall nev'r see again) might be a happy year to all my kind readers.

I am, your faithful servant,
R. Saunders

Appendix B

"Dialogue with the Gout" and Madame Brillon

In October of 1780 Benjamin Franklin, having consigned himself to the Passy estates near Paris, France, suffered an agonizing attack of gout. Painful though it was, his humor could not restrain writing an amusing retort to a teasing poem penned by one of his many lady friends.

Madame Anne-Louise Boyvin d' Hardancourt Brillon de Jouy was a light in Ben's life at that time, as were most of the Parisian ladies.

Even so, at the age of 74 he was thought more a paternal figure than the suitor he wished to be.

Still, many of the French ladies delighted in perching upon his ample lap, while sharing a bit of sexual banter. They would then leap up and laughingly run off, leaving poor Ben flushed with an erotic ardor.

But Madame Brillon, a 36-year-old married mother of two daughters, was different. To her, the man she had come to know and adore since 1777 was emotionally an adopted father. Her own father had recently passed away and she regarded the dependable Franklin in the role.

Ben, preferring to function as a consort could not visualize himself in this protective state, but finally conceded to her plea.

"For you have taken in my heart," she had written to him, "the place of that father whom I loved and respected so much [1]."

Having no desire to lose her friendship, nor the possibility of a future affair, he replied:

"I accept with infinite pleasure, my dear friend, your kind offer to adopt me as your father. I would be most happy to be the parent of such a good child... Yes, my dear child, I love you as a father, with all my heart. It is a truth that I sometime suspect this heart of wanting to go further. But I try to hide this from myself... This draws sighs from me, for which I do not reproach myself, because even at my age it is not becoming to say that I am in love with a young woman, there is nothing which prevents me from confessing that I admire and love my daughter because she is truly lovable, and because she loves me."

Madame Brillon, now assuming the role of his daughter, refused Ben any further ardent advances, yet was vehement in her jealousy affecting his attention paid other ladies, often admonishing him his "lack of will when you meet with the opposite sex."

Her little poem, in which "Madam Gout" alludes to this as a partial source for his torment, had Ben reeling with laughter; reducing him to lie prone, his feet propped to relieve the pain.

Unable to settle for sleep that night, he composed one of his wittiest essays:

Benjamin Franklin's
"Dialogue with the Gout"
B.F.:

> **Eh! Oh! Eh! What have I done to merit these cruel sufferings?**

Gout:

> **Many things; you have ate and drank too freely, and too much indulg'd those legs of yours in their indolence.**

B.F.:

> **Who is it that accuses me?**

Gout:

> **It is I, even I, the Gout.**

B.F.:

> **What! My enemy in person?**

Gout:

> **No, not your enemy.**

B.F.:

> **I repeat; my enemy; for you would not only torment my body to death, but ruin my good name; you reproach me as a glutton**

and a tippler; now all the world, that knows me, will allow that I am neither the one nor the other.

Gout:

The world may think as it pleases; it is always very complaisant to itself, and sometimes to its friends; but I very well know that the quantity of meat and drink proper for a man, who takes a reasonable degree of exercise, would be too much for another, who never takes any.

B.F.:

I take... Eh! Oh! ...as much exercise... Eh! ...as I can, Madam Gout. You know my sedentary state, and on that account, it would seem, Madam Gout, as if you might spare me a little, seeing it is not altogether my own fault.

Gout:

Not a jot; your rhetoric and your politeness are thrown away; your apology avails nothing. If your situation in life is a sedentary one, your amusement, your recreations, at least, should be active. You ought to walk or ride;or, if the weather prevents that, play at billiards. But let us examine your course of life. While the mornings are long, and you have leisure to go abroad, what do you do? Why, instead of gaining an appetite for breakfast, by salutary exercise, you amuse

yourself with books, pamphlets, or newspapers, which commonly are not worth the
reading. Yet you eat an inordinate breakfast, four dishes of tea, with cream, and one
or two buttered toasts, with slices of hung
beef, which I fancy are not things the most
easily digest'd. Immediately afterward you
sit down to write at your desk, or converse
with persons who apply to you on business.
Thus the time passes till one, without any
kind of exercise. But all this I could pardon,
in regards, as you say, to your sedentary
condition. But what is your practice after
dinner? Walking in the beautiful gardens
with those friends, with whom you din'd, as
would be the choice of men of sense; yours is
to be fix'd down to chess, where you are
found engag'd for two or three hours! This
is your perpetual recreation, which is the
least eligible of any for a sedentary man, because, instead of accelerating the motions of
the fluids, the rigid attention it requires to
retard the circulation and obstruct internal
secretions. Wrapt in the speculations of this
wretch'd game, you destroy your constitution. What can be expect'd from such a
course of living but a body replete with stag-
nant humours, ready to fall a prey to all
kinds of dangerous maladies, if I, the Gout,
did not occasionally bring you relief by agi-

tating those humours, and so purifying or dissipating them? If it was in some nook or alley in Paris, depriv'd of walks, that you play'd awhile at chess after dinner, this might be excusable; but the same taste prevails with you in Passy, Auteuil, Montmartre, or Sanoy, places where there are the finest gardens and walks, pure air, beautiful women, and most agreeable and instructive conversation; all which you might enjoy by frequenting the walks. But these are reject'd for this abominable game of chess. Fie, then Mr. Franklin! But amidst my instructions, I had almost forgot to administer my wholesome corrections; so take that twinge... And that...

B.F.:

Oh! Ehhh!!! It's not fair to say I take no exercise, when I do very often, going out to dine and returning in my carriage.

Gout:

That, of all imaginable exercises, is the most slight and insignificant, if you allude to the motion of a carriage suspend'd on many springs. By observing the degree of heat obtain'd by different kinds of motion, as we may form an estimate of the quantity of exercise given by each. Thus, for an example, if you turn out to walk in winter with cold feet, in an hour's time you will be in a glow all over; ride on horseback, the same effect will scarcely be perceiv'd by four hours' round trotting; but if you roll in a carriage, such as you have mention'd, you may travel all day and gladly enter the last inn to warm your feet by a fire. Flatter yourself then no longer, that half an hour's airing in your carriage deserves the name of exercise. Providence has appoint'd few to roll in carriages, while He has given all a pair of legs.

B.F.:

How can you so cruelly sport with my torment?

Gout:

Sport! I am very serious. I have here a list of offenses against your own health distinctly written, and can justify every stroke inflict'd on you.

B.F.:

Read it then.

Gout:

It is too long a detail; but I will briefly mention some particulars.

B.F.:

Proceed. I am all attention.

Gout:

Do you remember how often you have promis'd yourself, the following morning, a walk in the grove of Boulogne, in the garden de la Muette, or in your own garden, and have violated your promise, alleging, at one time, it was too cold, at another too warm, too windy, too moist, or what else you pleas-'d; when in truth it was too nothing, but your insuperable love of ease?

B.F.:

That I confess may have happen'd occasionally, probably ten times a year.

Gout:

Your confession is very far short of the truth; I say the gross amount is one hundred and ninety-nine times.

B.F.:

Is it possible?

Gout:

So possible, that it is a fact; you may rely on the accuracy of my statement. You know M. Brillon's gardens, what fine walks they contain; you know the handsome flight of an hundred steps, which lead from the terrace above to the lawn below. You have been in the practice of visiting this amiable family twice a week, after dinner, and it is a maxim of your own, that "a man may take as much exercise in walking a mile, up and down the stairs, as in ten on level ground." What an opportunity was here for you to exercise in both these ways! Did you embrace it, and how often?

B.F.:

I cannot immediately answer that question.

Gout:

I will do it for you; not once.

B.F.:

Not once?

Gout:

Even so. During the summer you went there at six o'clock. You found the charming lady, with her lovely children, eager to walk with you, and entertain you, and what has been your choice? Why to sit on the terrace, satisfying yourself with its fine prospect, and passing your eye over the beauties of the garden below, without taking one step to descend and walk about them. On the contrary, you call for tea and the chessboard; and lo! you are occupied in your seat till nine o'clock, and that besides two hour's play after dinner; and then, instead of walking home, which would have bestirr'd you a little, you step into your carriage...

B.F.:

What then would you have me do with my carriage?

Gout:

Burn it if you choose; you would at least get the heat out of it in this way; or, if you dislike that proposal here's another for you; observe the poor peasants, who work in the vineyards and grounds about the villages of Passy, Auteuil, Chaillot, &c.; you may find every day, among these deserving creatures, four or five old men and women, bent and perhaps crippl'd by weight of years, and too long and too great labour. After a most fatiguimg day, these people have to trudge a mile or two to their smoky huts. Order your coachman to set them down. This is an act that will be good for your soul; and, at the same time, after your visit to the Brillons, if you return on foot, that will be good for your body.

B.F.:

Ah! How tiresome you are!

Gout:

Well, then, to my office; it should not be forgott'n that I am your physician. There...

B.F.:

Ohhh! What a devil of a physician!

Gout:

How ungrateful you are to say so! Is it not I who, in the character of your physician, have sav'd you from the palsy, dropsy, and apoplexy! One or other of which would have done for you long ago, but for me.

B.F.:

I submit, and thank you for the past, but entreat the discontinuance of your visits for the future; for, in my mind, one had better

die than be cur'd so dolefully... Oh! Oh!...
For heaven's sake leave me, and I promise
faithfully never more to play at chess, but to
exercise daily, and live temperately.

Gout:

I know you too well. You promise fair;
but, after a few months of good health, you
will return to your old habits; your fine promises will be forgott'n like the forms of last
year's clouds. Let us then finish the account,
and I will go. But I leave you with an assur-
ance of visiting you again at a proper time
and place; for my object is for your good,
and you are sensible now that I am your
REAL FRIEND.

A few days later, laughing to himself as we might picture it, Ben handed his courier Madame Brillon's poem and
his essay, along with this crafty little note:

"One of the characters of your fable, Madame la Goutte
[Madam Gout], seems to me to reason pretty well, except
when she supposes that mistresses have had a share in producing this painful malady. I, for one, think the contrary;
and here is my reasoning: When I was a young man and
enjoy'd more of the favours of the fair sex than at present, I
had no gout at all. Hence, if the ladies of Passy had shown
more of that Christian charity, which I have so often recom-
mend'd to you in vain, I should not have gout now. I think
this to be very logical."

Her response?

On November 18, 1780, the venerable Dr. Franklin received this frizzled bit of logic:

"For me, nothing remains but the faculty of my loving friends. You do not doubt, surely, that I will do my best for you, in the spirit of Christian charity — but to the exclusion of <u>your</u> brand of Christian charity.

Your Affectionate Daughter,
B."

By 1782, Ben would resign himself to the consummate "papa" image Madame Brillon had longed for.

When she discovered her husband was having an affair with the governess of their children, she therefore turned her distressed head to the one person she felt she could now trust:

"My dear papa... Mademoiselle J------ [Jupin], forever extolling virtues which she never practiced, a delicacy she herself knew nothing of, a frankness she does not possess, was clever enough, after being disowned by her family, and expelled from two households, to take advantage of me to such an extent as to make all her adventures turn out to her credit; so much so that I pitied her, loved her, and always refused to listen to the repeated warnings I received to beware of her character.

"I almost paid with my life the ingratitude, the frightful evil, the falsity with which she deceived me. My husband will be perhaps for a long time under her spell; but I dare hope that my eagerness to please him, the affection of his children, the contempt which all our old and good friends have conceived for that girl and which they are not prepared

138

to conceal, will open his eyes some day. Meanwhile, I surrender entirely to the cleverness she will display in trying to
make me appear as ridiculous as possible.

"I beg that you keep my secret within your soul; keep
my heart there, too. I deposit it with you to heal it from its
wounds and weakness…"

The following letter, in reply to this abased young woman of so long ago, is as wise as any ever written since:

"You told me, my dear daughter, that your heart is too
sensitive. I see, by your letter, that that is true. To be very
sensitive to our own faults is good because it leads us to
avoid them in the future; but to be very sensitive to, and afflict'd by, the faults of others is not good. It is up to them
to be sensitive, and to be afflict'd, by what they have done
badly; for us, we must preserve the tranquility, which is the
just portion of innocence and virtue. But you say that 'ingratitude is a frightful evil.' It is true for the ungrateful —
but not for their benefactors. You have conferr'd acts of
kindness on those people you have thought worthy of them;
you have thus done your duty, since it is our duty to do this
good and you should be satisfi'd by it and be happy in the
reflection. If they are ungrateful it is their crime and not
yours; and it is up to them to be unhappy when they reflect
on the baseness of their conduct toward you. If they insult
you, think that although they could formally have been your
equals, they have, in this manner, plac'd themselves below
you; if you take revenge by punishing them, you therefore
restore them to their state of equality, which they lost. But
if you forgive them with no punishment, you keep them
fix'd in that low state into which they have fall'n, and from

which they can never escape without repentance and full reparation.

"Then follow, my very dear and always amiable daughter, the good resolution which you have so wisely made, to continue to fulfill all your duties as a good mother, good wife, good friend, good neighbour, &c. and ignore and forget, if you can, the insults you receive at present; and be asur'd that, given time, the rectitude of your conduct will prevail upon the minds of even the worst people, and still more on the minds of those people whose nature is basically good, and who also are endow'd with common sense, even tho', at present, they are led astray by the artifices of others. Then, everyone will quickly ask for the return of your friendship and will become, in the future, some of your most zealous friends.

"I am sensitive to the fact that I have just writt'n some very bad French; that could disgust you, you who write this charming language with so much purity and elegance. But, if you can finally decipher my awkward and improper expressions, you will have at least the kind of pleasure deriv'd from explaining riddles or discovering secrets.

Your always affectionate 'papa',
B.F."

In 1785, now suffering from painful bladder stones, Ben announced his plans to return home to America for a long needed rest. Permission to withdraw from his post as Minister to France had been granted by Congress on May 2nd, with Thomas Jefferson appointed his replacement. "I am only his successor," remarked Jefferson in accepting the position. "No one can replace him."

On July 9th, he met with Madame Brillon in his apartments for the last time.

On the afternoon of July 12th, he left the Passy estates "…in the midst," recorded Benjamin Bache [2], "of a very great concourse of the people of Passy; a mournful silence reigned around him, and was only interrupt'd by sobs." The queen's litter, borne by two large mules, carried him gently along the flower-strewn roads to the port city of Le Havre, where he would cross the English Channel to Southampton, then home to the country and people he yearned to see once more before he died.

In his pocket reposed two treasures. One was a parting gift from Louis XVI — a miniature portrait of the French king, encircled with 408 diamonds. The other, a neatly folded piece of paper, was prized even more:

"I could not bring myself to bid you a final farewell, my good friend. My heart was so overflowing on leaving you [on July 9th] that I feared that you and for me another such grievous experience would only add to the deep sorrow to which this separation causes me, without adding a further proof of the tender and unalterable friendship that I have pledged to you for all time.

"Every day of my existence memory reminds me that a great man, a sage, once deigned to be my friend. My very thoughts accompany him everywhere he goes. My heart mourns him unceasingly; unceasingly I shall say, always: 'Eight years I spent in the company of Docr. Franklin. They are passed and I shall never see them more.' Nothing in the world can ever console me for that loss,unless it be the conviction of that peace and happiness you must experience in the bosom of your family, and that fame which you surely enjoy in the land that owes you its liberty.

"O my friend, my good friend! I pray you may be happy. Tell me that you are, let me hear from you, and if it be sweet for you to recall the woman who loved you most dearly, think of all those members of my family who were and always must be your best friends.

"Good-bye, my heart fails me, it cannot bear being torn asunder from you, but you shall always be, my loving papa.
B."

To this M. Brillon, having been forgiven by his wife and restored to his own family bosom, penned this brief post-script:

"My very dear papa! I have nothing more to add; and even if I wanted to, my tears would not let me see."

Appendix C

Home to Rest

On September 14, 1785, the celebrated ship *London Packet* anchored off the Philadelphia shore. Ben was home at last. In his journal, he wrote: "My son-in-law [Richard Bache] came with a boat for us; we land'd at Market Street wharf, where we were receiv'd by crowds of people with huzzas, and accompanied with acclamations quite to my door. Found my family well."

To this last entry, he added: "God be prais'd and thank'd for all his mercies."

If Ben had thought he was really home to rest, though, he was sadly mistaken. Within a month he was pressed into service as president of the Pennsylvania Supreme Executive Council. "They have eat'n my flesh," he wrote to a friend, "and [now] seem resolv'd to pick my bones." When his sister Jane reproached him for accepting the seat "at your age," he candidly replied "We all have wisdom enough to judge what others ought to do, or not to do in the management of their affairs; and 'tis possible that I might blame you as much if you were to accept the offer of a young husband, at your age."

In February of 1786 he answered a letter from Bishop Shipley, who had anxiously inquired the condition of his health:

"I reciev'd lately your kind letter of Nov. 27th. My reception here was, as you have heard, very honourable indeed; but I was betray'd by it, and by some remains of ambition, from which I had imagin'd myself free, to accept the chair of government for the state of Pennsylvania, when the proper thing for me was repose and a private life. I hope to be able to bear the fatigue for one year, then to retire."

This was not to be, however. He was re-elected for two additional one-year terms, with only one vote cast against him each time, his own.

By 1787, at the age of 81, Ben was too old and ailing to call up energies paramount throughout his entrepreneurial career. Still, slowed though he was, he attended every function necessary to his office and continued expressing idealisms appropriate to a budding nation. One delegate to the Federal Convention, meeting him for the first time, later wrote "Docr. Franklin…is…a most extraordinary man, and tells a story in a style more engaging than anything I ever heard… He is eighty-two [sic] and possesses an activity of mind equal to a youth of twenty-five years of age."

Nevertheless, true age was taking its toll. In January of 1788 a severe fall down the stone steps of his garden ushered in the end. Subsequent months of increased suffering prepared his thoughts for death and he made out his will, which was officially signed and witnessed on July 17th. Friends urged him to finish the autobiographical script he had begun in 1771, but the opium he was absorbing to ease the excruciating pain of injuries, gout and bladder stones, made it too difficult. He would place the work carefully into the top drawer of his desk, incomplete [1].

Rallying his health for a short time, this remarkable man performed his last public service as president for the **Pennsylvania Society for Promoting the Abolition of Slavery, and the relief of Free Negroes Unlawfully Held in Bondage**.

As far back as 1751, Ben had argued economic weaknesses to the institution of slavery and suggested establishing a school for Negroes in Philadelphia by 1758. But England, then the reigning government and profiting from the slave trade, ignored his reasoning and suggestion.

Now, in the year 1789, he would invoke help from the newly constituted government for support and funds "in the cause of abolition," presented in an "Address to the Publick" on November 19th. Less than three months later, on February 12, 1790, he petitioned the first Congress to declare the abolition of slavery "law of the land." Both appeals were unsuccessful, with that august body reporting on March 5th that they "have no authority to interfere with the internal affairs of the states."

Not until the 13th Amendment to abolish slavery was ratified on December 6, 1865 did the United States officially dissolve what Benjamin Franklin called "An institution initiat'd by greed, and forg'd in blood."

Ben's end was near.

Early in March, forced to relieve his pains again with the use of opium, he took to his bed. His body, "powerfully built to last a hundred years," was now emaciated from loss of appetite caused by the drug. "Little remains of me," he noted to a friend, "but a skeleton cover'd with skin." It seems neither pain nor drug could effect his ready wit.

Thomas Jefferson, back from France to take his post as President Washington's secretary of state, visited Ben at his bedside. "[I] called on the venerable and beloved Franklin," he penned in his memoirs. "He was on the bed of sickness from which he never rose. My recent return from a country in which he had left so many friends, and the convulsions [French Revolution] to which they had been exposed, revived all his anxieties to know what part they had taken, what had been their course, and what their fate. He went over all in succession, with a rapidity and animation almost too much for his strength [2]."

On April 1st, Ben's condition worsened. His temperature rose dangerously, while his breathing abated to near suffocation. He remained in this state until the 8th, when he seemed to recover. On the 12th, he got up to have his bed made so that "I might die in a decent manner." When Sally hinted he looked well enough to live for several more years, he winked at his daughter and quipped, "I hope not." Five days later an abscess on his lungs burst and he slipped silently into a coma. Attending physician, Dr. John Jones, sadly recorded his passing in the black-bordered issue #3125 of the *Pennsylvania Gazette* the following day. "On the 17th instant," the notification read, "about eleven o'clock at night Benjamin Franklin quietly expired, closing a long and useful life of eighty-four years and three months."

On Wednesday afternoon, April 21st, a funeral procession gathered at the home of Richard and Sarah Bache and moved slowly up to Philadelphia's State House, then proceeded to Christ Church Burial Ground on the southeast corner of 5th and Arch Streets. The city's clergy, followed by distinguished citizens and the pall-covered coffin, solemnly led the cortege. Muffled bells tolled along the route. Flags were hung at half-mast.

He was lowered beside his wife and little Francis Folger to the discharge of ceremonial minute guns. The Rev. Dr. William Smith, provost of the College of Philadelphia, gave the eulogy, as an estimated twenty thousand mourners looked on. There was no rain that day, yet moisture pervaded the air.

Ben Franklin had come home to rest.

James Charles Bouffard, Psy.D., Ph.D.

"An investment in knowledge pays the best interest."
Benjamin Franklin
(1706 – 1790)

Appendix D

In Commemoration

To take leave of a man like Benjamin Franklin is to do so with infinite regret. He was indeed a grand personage, whose memory has been revered for the more than two hundred years since his passing.

Even so, covetous detractors emerged during the 19th and early 20th centuries. Figures well-known in their own right, such as the writers Nathaniel Hawthorne, Herman Melville, D.H. Lawrence, Charles Angoff and humorist Mark Twain, found ridicule in the adulation of Franklin and attempted to distort his image. The arrogant Melville, for example, saw him as "altogether of that race of men who are keen observers of the main chance. Thus, his greatness."

Jealousy has a venomous pen.

Benjamin Franklin achieved not his greatness from timely opportunities ["the main chance"], but from a magnitude within his own mind and will. At any time and place he would have distinguished himself; as his talents, strengths, admitted weaknesses, wit and grace culminated into a perfect man for any age.

Nathaniel Hawthorne assailed *Poor Richard's* as "all with respect to getting money, or saving it."

Franklin, the consummate businessman,would have concurred. "A penny sav'd is a penny earn'd," he would have answered the short-story author and novelist, who found it formidable to hold two coins at one time in a single pocket.

The brilliantly demented English novelist, poet and playwright, D.H. Lawrence, blamed Ben for everything he detested in himself, in America, and in the human race. "I cannot stand Benjamin," he scribbled rather illogically, "because he tries to take away my dark forest, my freedom."

Though Lawrence admitted admiration for Franklin during bouts of clarity, his obsession over the doctor's posthumous acclaim led, in part, to a premature death at the age of 45.

Mark Twain was harsh in his humor when he wrote in 1870: "...he [Franklin] ought to have been foraging for soap-fat and making candles."

Twain, himself self-educated and self-made, would halfway recant this statement in another paragraph, "Benjamin Franklin did a great many notable things for this country, and made her young name to be honored in many lands as

150

the mother of such a son," yet still leaned toward his conviction that Franklin's popular autobiography "...as a guidance to youth [is] a thing which has brought affliction to millions of boys since, whose fathers had read Franklin's pernicious biography."

The iconic author of *The Adventures of Tom Sawyer* and *Huckleberry Finn* undoubtedly referred to the second portion of the publicly favored autobiography, written while at the Passy Estates in 1784, in which Ben spoke of his own heroic deeds in an effort to inspire young hopefuls beginning life with no advantage but that of ability and character.

"I merely desired," explained a frustrated Twain when asked why his bitterness toward Franklin's autobiography, "to do away with somewhat of the calamitous idea among heads of families that Franklin acquired his great genius by working for nothing, studying by moonlight, and getting up in the night instead of waiting till morning like a Christian."

Perhaps this self-styled censor should have considered an assessment of Ben's autobiography by the mid-19th century French literary critic, Charles Augustin Sainte-Beuve, before subjecting himself to his own brand of ridicule from an agitated press:

> **Franklin's memoirs are full of interest for all those who have had a toilsome early life, and have experienced the difficulties of existence and the lack of generosity in men, but who are, nevertheless, not embittered, nor spoiled, nor fallen into the corruption and intrigues of self-interest; to all such, and to all whom the same circumstances await,**

these memoirs are a source of observation that will always be applicable, and of truth that will always be felt.

And Dr. Charles Angoff, an English Literature professor and author, told us that Ben "...represented the least praiseworthy qualities of the inhabitants of the New World; miserliness, fanatical practicality, and lack of interest in what are usually known as spiritual things."

Of the allegations heard thus far, Angoff's statement beclouds the true measure of Benjamin Franklin beyond reasoning. For such a learned individual to display the least perceptiveness whether from envy or from deficient examination of a subject is pitiable.

Benjamin Franklin cared little for his own personal possessions and achievements. Of inspiration and benefit to a world he would leave behind, he dedicated his life.

May we, as a whole, follow his example till the end of time?

Adieu, Ben Franklin my friend, until we meet again.

Notes

Prologue

1. "Good man" [French]

The Story:
Birth to Retirement

1. Unfortunately for history, this house was entirely consumed by fire on December 29, 1810, as flaming embers leapt to its roof from a burning livery stable cornered on Hawley Street. The building currently covering Ben's birthplace is a national monument containing a commemorative bust of the philosopher.

2. Although time proved Cotton Mather's endorsement of smallpox inoculations correct, both he and his father Increase did not like being crossed.

3 *The New-England Courant* continued publishing under the guise of Benjamin Franklin as editor and publisher until its demise in 1726.

4. Also called the *Annis* for its master, Thomas Annis.

5. Ben Franklin's favorite word for the mistakes in his life.

6. These points have been updated from Ben Franklin's original spelling.

7. Rogers had fooled Deborah, her friends, and apparently her mother, into believing he was a prosperous businessman. Though most potters did excellent business, he was never out of debt. In 1728 he escaped to, and later died in, the West Indies.

8. He and Thomas Denham were ill at the same time. In 1790, at the age of 84, he died of the pleurisy that had almost taken his life as a young man.

9. The Junto [pronounced Who-n-toe], founded by Ben Franklin in 1727 shortly after returning to Philadelphia from London, was business, politically and socially oriented and the nucleus of today's American Philosophical Society.

10. Keimer fled to Barbados, where he took employment as a printer for one of his former employees and died a poor man.

11. Coarse linen.

12. The Gregorian calendar. Named for Pope Gregory XIII [pope, 1572-85], who first introduced a correct-

ed form of the Julian calendar in 1582. Benjamin Franklin, obeying a decree of England's King George II, would herald it to the colonies in 1751 for the year 1752. [See **Appendix A.**]

13. Mother, with Holy Roman Emperor Franz I, of Marie Antoinette, Queen of France. [Born Maria Antonia Josepha Johanna in Austria on November 2, 1755. Guillotined on October 16, 1793 during the French Revolution's "Reign of Terror," 1793-94].

14. Although the Franklin stove was manufactured by the Warwick Furnace Company in 1742, and widely advertised in 1744, official records disclose it was devised in 1740.

15. A dealer in hardware [England].

16. A tube charged with electricity through the use of a Leyden jar.

Appendix B
"Dialogue with the Gout" and Madame Brillon

1. Letters and the essay are translated from their original French.
2. Ben Franklin's grandson who, with William Temple, accompanied him to France.

Appendix C
Home to Rest

1. Benjamin Franklin's incomplete autobiography ends with his mission to England in 1757.
2. Madame Brillon [born Anne-Louise Boyvin d' Hardancourt in Paris on December 13, 1744], a musical protégé, survived the French Revolution. When she died on December 5, 1824, at the age of 79, she had become the celebrated composer Benjamin Franklin had once told her she would.

Bibliography

The following represents but a small portion of the many books and papers [several that are rare] consulted during preparation of this work.

Aldridge, Alfred Owen. "Benjamin Franklin and the Pennsylvania Gazette." Proceedings of the American Philosophical Society, 1962.

Angoff, Charles. *A Literary History of the American People*. A.A. Knopf, New York, NY, 1931.

Benson, Mary S. *Women in Eighteenth-Century America*. Columbia University Press, New York, NY, 1935.

Blake, John W. "The inoculations Controversy in Boston: 1721 – 1722." New England Quarterly, 1952.

Bloore, Steven. "Samuel Keimer: A Footnote to the Life of Franklin." Pennsylvania Magazine of History and Biography, 1930. [Hereafter cited as P.M.H.B.]

Boorston, Daniel. *The Americans: The Colonial Experience*. Random House, New York, NY, 1958.

Bridenbaugh, Carl. *Cities in the Wilderness*. A.A. Knopf, New York, NY, 1960.

Bruce, William Cabell. *Benjamin Franklin, Self-Revealed*. 2 vols. G.P. Putnam's Sons, New York, NY, 1917.

Bushman, Richard L. *On the Uses of Psychology: Conflict and Conciliation in Benjamin Franklin*. Harvard University Press, Cambridge, MA, 1966.

Cohen, I. Bernard, Editor. *Benjamin Franklin's Experiments*. Harvard University Press, Cambridge, MA, 1941.

De Armond, Anna Janney. *Andrew Bradford, Colonial Journalist*. University of Delaware

Press, Newark, DE, 1949.

Eggleston, Edward. *A First Book in American History*. American Book Co., New York, NY, 1917.

Feldman, Eve. *Benjamin Franklin, Scientist and Inventor*. F. Watts, New York, NY, 1990.

Fennelly, Catherine. "William Franklin of New Jersey." William and Mary Quarterly, 1949. [Hereafter cited as W.M.Q.]

Franklin, Benjamin. *The Autobiography of Benjamin Franklin*. Various edited versions, 1887 – 1964.

Franklin, William Temple, Editor. *Memoirs of the Life and Writings of Benjamin Franklin*. 3 vols. London, 1817-18. [Note: Although the "Memoirs" are considered by some historians a reckless hodgepodge of mismatched information "doing Franklin more harm than good," the people of the 19th century discovered his true genius through this effort of his grandson.
Even John Adams, Benjamin Franklin's harshest critic, subsequent to reading the first volume was moved to write: "I rejoice

that the publick are to have a compleat [sic]
edition of his works, for there is scarce a
scratch of his pen that is not worth preserv-
ing." Actually, Temple managed to publish
only a small selection of the philosopher's
vast writings in 3 volumes. Within six years,
he was dead.]

Gray, Austin K. *The First American Library.*
Library Company of Philadelphia, Philadelphia, PA, 1936.

Hawthorne, Nathaniel. *Benjamin Franklin: A
Biographical Story.* Boston, MA, 1884.

Kenney, Robert W. "James Ralph: An Eight-
eenth Century Philadelphian in Grub Street."
P.M.H.B., April 1940.

Miller, Perry. *The New England Mind: From
Colony to Province.* Harvard University
Press, Cambridge, MA, 1940.

Parton, James. *The Life and Times of Benjamin Franklin.* 2 vols. Mason Brothers,
Boston, MA, 1864.

Ross, John F. "The Character of Poor Richard:
Its source and Alterations." Proceedings of
the Modern Language Association of Ameri-

ca, 1940.

Tolles, F.B. "Benjamin Franklin's Mentors: The Philadelphia Quaker Merchants." W.M. Q., January 1947.

Van Doren, Carl. *Benjamin Franklin*. The Viking Press, New York, NY, 1938.

Van Doren, Carl. *The Letters of Benjamin Franklin and Jane Mecom*. Princeton University Press, Princeton, NJ, 1950.

Warden, G.B. *Boston, 1689 — 1776*. Little, Brown and Company, Boston, MA, 1970.

Warner, Sam Bass. *The Private City: Philadelphia in Three Periods of its Growth*. University of Pennsylvania Press, Philadelphia, PA, 1968.

Wroth, Lawrence. *Benjamin Franklin: The Printer at Work*. The Franklin Institute, Philadelphia, PA, 1943.

Zall, Paul M. *Benjamin Franklin Laughing*. University of California Press, Los Angeles, CA, 1980.

James Charles Bouffard, Psy.D., Ph.D.

"All human situations have their inconveniences. We feel those of the present, but neither see nor feel those of the future; and hence we often make troublesome changes without amendment, and frequently for the worse."

Benjamin Franklin
(1706 – 1790)

"Do not fear mistakes. You will know failure. Continue to reach out."

Benjamin Franklin
(1706 – 1790)

Young Ben Franklin stands notice by the provincial governor of Pennsylvania, Sir William Keith, in 1723.
[Artwork from: *A First Book in American History* by Edward Eggleston (1837 – 1902). Publisher: American Book Company, New York ÷ Cincinnati ÷ Chicago, 1917 edition.]

Index

Page numbers with an italicized *n* are in the **Notes** section.

Index

Index

Index

Index

Index

Index

Index

The Entrepreneurial Ben Franklin

Index

Index

Index

Index

Index

Index

Index

Pennsylvania Gazette [1. **FRANKLIN and MERE-
DITH**'s newspaper], 50, 53 [2. **B. FRANKLIN**'s
newspaper], 53-54, 61, 70, 107, 111, 147
Pennsylvania General Assembly, Ben as clerk of, 76,
108
Pennsylvania Hospital, Ben founds, 110
Pennsylvania Militia [also see Associators, the], 83-84
**Pennsylvania Society for the Abolition of Slavery
and the Relief of Free Negroes Held in Bonage**,
Ben as president of, 119, 145
Pennsylvania Supreme Executive Council, Ben elected
president of, 118
Philadelphia:
   description of, 29-30
   Ben enters, 30, 106
   Ben begins working for Samuel Keimer in, 30-32
   Ben begins courting Deborah Read in, 31
   Ben stands notice by Provincial Governor Keith in,
      31
   Thomas Denham regains fortune in, 34
   Thomas Denham makes preparations for return to, 34
   Thomas Denham plans to open a new store in, 34
   Ben and Denham arrive in, 36
   Ben resumes courtship with Deborah Read Rogers
      in, 36-37
   Ben becomes merchant's clerk in, 37, 107
   Ben returns to printing trade in, 37
   Ben enters partnership with Hugh Meredith on
      [**FRANKLIN and MEREDITH**], 46-52, 107
   Ben becomes sole proprietor of printing business in
      [**B. FRANKLIN**], 53, 107
   Ben marries Deborah Read Rogers [com-
      mon-law ceremony] in, 54

Index

Index

Poor Robin's Almanack, 61
Pope, Alexander, 62
Pope's Creek Estate, 60
Postmaster General of North America, Ben appointed as, 111
Prescott, Samuel, 115
Privy Council, 112, 115
Proposals Relating to the Education of Youth in Pennsylvania, Ben first draws up, 109

Q

Quaker city, Philadelphia as, 29-30, 83
Quaker, Historie of the Rise, Increase, and Progress of the Christian People called [folio], 47
Quaker merchant, Peter Collinson as, 76
Quaker merchant, Thomas Denham as, 32
Quaker ruled Assembly, 83

R

Rabelais, Francois, 62
Race and Second Streets, Ben's post-retirement home in Philadelphia, 58
Ralph, James, 32-33, 42
Read [Rogers], Deborah, 31, 36, 41, 54, 154*n*
real estate, Ben's holdings in, 85
Revere, Paul, 115
Rhode Island [see Newport, Rhode Island]
Rogers, John, 36, 154*n*
Royal Society [London], Ben awarded the Copley Medal by, 110
Royal Society [London], Ben elected fellow of, 111

Index

S

T

Index

James Charles Bouffard, Psy.D., Ph.D.

"While we may not be able to control all that happens
to us, we can control what happens inside us."
Benjamin Franklin
(1706 – 1790)

About the Author

Dr. Bouffard holds an LL.B. from LaSalle University, a Masters and Psy.D. from Neotarian College of Psychology. And has applied thirty years to psychological counseling.

In 1999, he earned a Ph.D. (a candidacy shelved for twenty years due to time restraints).

His lifelong fascination with history has led him to currently author several papers and books in this genre.